Sean Gullette as Max Cohen

π

DARREN ARONOFSKY

faber and faber

First published in 1998
by Faber and Faber Limited
3 Queen Square London WC1N 3AU

Published in the United States by Faber and Faber, Inc.,
a division of Farrar, Straus and Giroux, Inc., New York

Photoset by Parker Typesetting Service, Leicester
Printed in England by Mackays of Chatham plc, Chatham, Kent

Photo credits:
Photographs on pages i, 73, 77, 80, 88, 103, 107, 123
© Matthew Libatique;
pages 34, 35, 142 © Sue Johnson;
pages 2, 7, 16 © Darren Aronofsky;
pages 14, 22, 41 © Ariyela Wald-Cohain;
pages 17 (sketch), 18, 29, 30, 64, 66, 118, 150 © Matthew Maraffi;
pages 56, 60 © David Gullette;
pages 62, 111 © Katie King

A CIP record for this book
is available from the British Library

ISBN 0-571-20042-7

2 4 6 8 10 9 7 5 3 1

To my parents,
to their health, to their happiness –

CONTENTS

January 31, 1996–January 14, 1998:

The Guerilla Diaries

Darren Aronofsky

PRE-PRODUCTION

Just got back from Sundance and I'm feeling amazingly restored. I badly want to believe that if you make *your own* film and you make it well, it will get recognized. It may not be Sundance Competition – or even Sundance Midnight – but the film will find its audience.

Some of this year's films were homemade and truly original. Eric Watson and I now have the courage to move forward with a feature film project. We've been talking about shooting a guerrilla film by all means necessary – serious talk for a recovering slacker like me, but momentum is building.

We want to make a film for $20,000. That's how much we figure we can raise for sure. At Sundance we saw *Tokyo Fist*, by cyberpunk master Shinya Tsukamoto. I admire his passion and fierce fucking originality. I want to bring cyberpunk to America. Cronenberg did it in Canada but no one has pulled it off in the States, especially not in NYC, where these ideas fit the environment perfectly.

My twenty-seventh birthday is twelve days away. I can see new lines on my face in the mirror. I'm not a kid anymore – and I haven't shot film in a long time.

I have a list of seven projects in various stages of development. I studied them all from the point of view of a possible guerrilla production. *Dreamland*, my focus for the past eighteen months, is a $2,000,000 project, and this kind of funding is nowhere in sight. The others have similar problems of scale.

I've got one possibility. The working title is 'Chip in the

3

Head'. Along with the title I have a single image of Sean Gullette, my actor friend from college, standing in front of the mirror, his head shaved bald, digging into his skull with an X-Acto blade for an implant he thinks is in there.

The other thing that attracts me to the idea is the memory of the first film I did in undergrad school. We were given 400 feet of black and white reversal and told to do a portrait film on a single character. I like the idea of a portrait film, a character study, to control my palette. Sean would be great for this film. He's so edgy, so charismatic, and very focused. For years we've talked about collaborating on a project that would use all of our creative energies.

FEBRUARY 12, 2.16AM: THE CALL TO ADVENTURE

I'm twenty-seven today. The heat in my cockroach-infested tenement in Hell's Kitchen has finally been turned on. The heat on my life has been turned on as well.

I took Sean to dim sum in Chinatown and over shrimp dumplings I asked him if he'd be willing to star in and help create this new project. I told him deep collaboration would be a very hard journey – many times we'd want to kill each other – but when it was all over we'd have something special.

Sean took a moment to think and then his mind started firing. I could see that he was legitimately excited. His magazine, *KGB*, is running into hard times and its future is unclear. He needs to get back to acting, and he was also psyched about collaborating with me, which we haven't done since *Supermarket Sweep*, in college. He liked the idea of a portrait film and reminded me of a short animated film my college room-mate Dan Schrecker made. It was called *Ren Chi Ren*, which means 'Man Eats Man' in Chinese. Sean did the voice-over for this brilliant animated short about a homeless man who started to think everyone around him is a cannibal.

I'm also inspired by a book that was submitted to my friend Colson Whitehead at the *Voice Literary Supplement*, where he edits. It is a crudely self-published conspiracy theory book written by what I would call a legitimate paranoid schizophrenic. This guy sees numerical connections between truly random systems (i.e. the model of JFK's car and the date Martin Luther King met Marilyn Monroe). I think the narrator of this book is a good starting point for Sean's character. The only problem is that he is insane. Will an audience buy a crazy, paranoid hero for ninety minutes?

FEBRUARY 15, 9.45PM: THE GOOD, THE BAD AND THE UGLY

Eric Watson is a great collaborator. We met the first week at film school in LA. He grew up in San Fran, I grew up in Brooklyn, but we were both from similar hip-hop upbringings. At AFI (American Film Institute), I used to make fun of his musical tastes, because he was into the early electronic music scene. Little did I know electronica was on its way to replacing hip-hop as the new underground. Eric has what some would call an 'old soul'. He listens and has wisdom, and he can probably form an accurate impression of someone quicker than any human I know.

Sean Gullette is also a great collaborator, but for different reasons. He has a raw, edgy talent and an unequaled work ethic. He is wickedly brilliant and ultimately a complete original. In contrast to Eric, Sean is a 'new soul' because many of his ideas are so outside of the norm that some would call him ridiculous, while others would call him genius. Sean's willing to take any chance with his body and emotions and for me, as a director of a no-budget film, this will be very, very important. I will know that I have him one hundred percent.

I believe the three of us will make a firm base for this monster collaboration. A triangle holding up a giant circle. Our personalities blend and contrast enough so that the most obvious weaknesses are covered. If any of us stumble, we'll have two friends to pick us up. I know all this may sound soft, but the fact is that nothing can make up for creative partners. I spent many years struggling by myself to push the bus over the hill, but with partners I'll be damned if that crest ain't coming soon. And then – besides some potholes and bumps – it's all downhill.

FEBRUARY 23, 2.19PM: PIZZA AND FALAFEL

I am dying from greasy food. It sucks. Eric and I share this shitbag apartment in Manhattan's whore district. When we moved in we busted a john getting his dick sucked by some junky. They were embarrassed and nice; Eric was friendly; I was furious.

I'm working at my sister Patti's apartment on 11th Street in the daytime while she's at work at CBS News. Powerbook, index cards, bottle of water, a window overlooking midday traffic on 4th Avenue.

Two big ideas in the last week. First, on the problem of the audience not relating to a crazy person: I spun Sean's character into a mathematician and I named him Maximilian. The name is strong. The occupation is right. The film is about a man who sees numerical patterns in his world. Everywhere he looks he sees numbers. The only way an audience will buy this character will be if he's a math genius.

But there's a new problem: in this life, Sean is a literary genius, not a math genius. I've got the genius thing but suckerboy can't multiply 9 by 7. His written numbers look like chicken scrawl. I guess this is where acting enters. Sean will find a way to do it.

The π-ing of New York.

The second brainstorm was the title of the film. I want to call the movie π. When the idea came to me it made so much sense. Plus it's a great marketing angle. I can see it now: πs everywhere – stenciled on buildings and street corners, billboards, napkins, match books, beer coasters.

I'm super excited because a symbol hasn't been used for a movie title. It will make people think and that's what π is going to be. People will see the symbol and say, 'What's that?' Then the hook is in and we just need to give them the info for how to get to the theater.

Yeah, but – will π ever make it to the theater? I don't know. The ideas I have circling are really out there. I know that we will execute them well and I know that at the core of the film will be a driving, vibrant thriller but it's going to be weird and bugged out. When we talk about the future, we know we're aiming for a slot in Sundance Midnight and hopefully a run at the Film Forum, a smaller, respectable art house. The Angelika is out of the question. It's controlled by the big distributors like Miramax and October and they'll probably laugh at the film.

If we can't get a run at the Forum it means a nightmare of self-distribution, but I want to get my investors' money back. That's the one back-end requirement and I will do that no matter what. Even if it means minimum wage at Kinko's.

MARCH 18, 5.39PM: PARANOIA

A thought from today: Writing movies is like reverse paranoia. Paranoids see signs of a hidden order behind reality. When you write a movie you construct a world of signs which all point to the protagonist. The result is a fictional world which mirrors the world of paranoids. In fact, this may mean that Americans who spend hours in movies think that everything is going to work out and everything has an ordered purpose, like a Hollywood script. But the reality is that things don't work out and everything is chaotic. Hollywood films have turned America into a land of paranoids. We must 'fight paranoia with paranoia'.

APRIL 3, 4.13PM: WEST SIDE HIGHWAY

It's Passover and Sean, me and my pop are in the car on the way to Brooklyn for dinner at my parents' house. We've been working on π pretty seriously and things are going all right. These things are so hard to work on. You sit there, you make the time, you get tired and don't want to move ahead, but move ahead is what you must do. The sun is setting over Jersey City in a classic smog-filled sunset – shattering oranges, rich yellows, unrealistic purples and the ringing truth of putrid green. On Friday I leave for the Catskills, where I'll do a bunch of writing at Dan Schrecker's parents' pad.

APRIL 5, 7.20PM: CROSSING THE FIRST THRESHOLD

I am in the country at Marv and Ellen's place. Dan was nice enough to offer this cabin in bum-fuck nowhere. It's freezing cold and snowing outside. The nearest neighbor is two miles away and there's no TV or stereo. Just a fire. I've located a copy of Stephen King's *Carrie*, but I'm trying not to read it and focus on the work.

I am here to write the first draft of π. Sean, Eric and I have brainstormed for the last few months and I believe I have enough to put some scenes to paper. Alien abductions have turned into mad Pythagorean monks spying in the streets of Manhattan, which in turn transformed into a Hasidic kabbalah sect. The latter is perfect for a mathematician, because the biblical codes are all about numbers. Also, the Hasids will look good in black and white.

My knowledge of the kabbalah stems from a trip I took to Israel when I was seventeen. I graduated high school early and decided to go to Europe for six months. I then volunteered for a kibbutz in northern Israel with the dream that I'd be in a field picking avocados with beautiful Scandinavian girls. In reality, I was placed in a plastic factory, working two assembly lines at once for eight hours a day. The timing was set so that I was literally running for eight hours.

Two days later I said fuck this and I ran away in the middle of the night. I hitched to Jerusalem and went straight to the Western Wall. Now, if you're seventeen and an assimilated American Jew hanging out in Jerusalem, it takes about thirty minutes until a yeshivah will approach you and offer you room and board in exchange for taking part in Torah study. Broke, and always open to something new, I took them up on the offer. For several days I was bombarded with a ton of kabbalah and other cool information, and saw Jerusalem in style. They weren't successful in converting me, but I was enlightened by some incredible stuff.

Enough procrastinating. In many ways this may prove the most important week of my life. These are the rules for this draft:

1 Always move forward. If you have a problem, type through it.
2 Only take a break after something good happens on the page or you accomplish a goal. No breaks for confusion: type through it.
3 Ten pages a day minimum.
4 Only go back to add something. Do not remove contradictions, just make a note.
5 Do it. Suffer, live, cry, struggle for one week. You'll feel like a million bucks by the fifteenth.
6 Have fun.

APRIL 6, 12.10AM: BROOKLYN BOY IN THE WOODS

Writing is going well but I stopped to read *Carrie*. Scared the fuck out of me. I'm really terrified. I think the nightmares are invading the draft.

APRIL 10, 12.29AM: OUTLAWS

I had a dream last night: Eric and I held up a bank with two other guys. Suddenly, it got bloody. One of our accomplices turned on us. I shot him. He kept coming. I shot him again, *splat*! He kept coming. It took five bullets finally to kill him but as he was falling to the ground he lunged at me and stabbed me with a small knife.

It didn't stop us. Eric and I jumped in a cab that was half car and half motorcycle. The back compartment was a normal cab but the front of the cab was the front of the motorcycle. The cabbie sat between Eric and I to operate the contraption. Eric wanted to go to Hell's Kitchen, but I told him it would be best to get lost in Brooklyn before we made a break for Mexico. The cabbie didn't want to take us to Brooklyn but I told him I'd give him a nice tip. I woke up.

Well, at least I was Clyde and Eric was Bonnie. Actually, it might be cooler to be Bonnie.

MAY 6, 12.24AM: PAIN

The fifty-three-page script feels strong. I will send it out to a select group of friends for feedback.

Sean and I continue to workshop every day at my sister's apartment. I have him doing personal journal entries in character. We're developing Max Cohen's backstory and we're rehearsing scenes. We've transformed Max's insomnia into migraines. An actor friend of mine, whom I've worked with for years, finally revealed to me that she's been suffering from vicious migraines for the past five years. They're so serious they've debilitated her and have really sidetracked her career. I've started to do research into attacks and Sean is doing his own work, reading Oliver Sachs' book and some medical texts. Migraine headaches are really spectacular and no one can explain them. I think they'll be excellent to portray on film. I'm intrigued by the cinematic possibilities.

We've decided to go for sync sound, but to limit it as much as possible. There's some strong dialogue in the script and we have to use it. The film is starting to come alive.

JULY 7, 4.18PM: WHO IS MAX COHEN?

OK, so the script seems to be getting good responses. People are excited. I do feel that it is ready to shoot. There may be some problems, but they will work themselves out in the process. Trying to make it happen for twenty Gs.

We both hate the voice-over as written, but I told Sean that we'll work on it after we film, when we know what we need.

We asked Jah for some guidance and he gave me a moment of light and I fused together Max's backstory. We started with Eric's past and upbringing as a launching pad. At some level, Max's past is Eric, Max's present is Sean, and Max's future is me.

I recognize so much of Max's loneliness and paranoia from my tortured existence in LA last year. The City of the Snake can be devilish for those alone and broke. I nearly left my brain in a wastepaper basket in my dingy pad in Hollywood, California.

AUGUST 2, 1.13AM: REFUSAL OF THE CALL

The film has been thrown into jeopardy by our now former director of photography, whom for privacy reasons we will call Chuckie Sellout. π just smacked hard into its first hurdle.

It happened like this. Both Eric and I sensed a feeling of

distance from Chuckie at the production meeting on Tuesday night. I guess the fact that he was more interested in flipping through a *Hollywood Reporter* than in participating in the meeting was a clear sign.

I called him Wednesday and told him we had to talk. I told him that I sensed that he wasn't giving π one hundred percent, and that I need a DP who is going to do so. He started by saying that he was upset that we weren't going to give him the $2,500 he wanted for his camera package. Originally, we had partly chosen him for his (free) camera package, but if he wants $2,500 I felt that we could somehow find the cash.

But then he dropped the bomb. He tells me that he is presently considering doing a 35mm film in September. Hold on, we're shooting in September. What the fuck? He tells me that he can't work on the tight schedule we have – what if he gets offered an episode of *Homicide*? Couldn't we push back a while, extend the schedule, shoot a few weekends?

Clearly that is unacceptable. I tell him that. He retreats for a moment and asks for a week to decide if he can dedicate to π. I'm thinking, 'You shook my hand four months ago and we've been developing a strategy to make the film with you for longer than that. Then, two weeks before we enter pre-production you get yellow.' I was furious, but I decided to hold all my cards and I left without an argument.

Cut to today. We're chilling with our editor Oren Sarch at *Palestrini Post*. I know that this collaborator is a partner: he understands the opportunity we have here. The phone rings. It's Chuckie and he wants to meet.

I take the express train downtown. He's delaying, postponing confrontation, and I see it coming. I focus on my breathing, like a good yoga student. We sit down. Then he says it: 'I can't commit.' All I wanted to do was tear out his treacherous throat, but I remained calm. I know that screaming, even though I had earned it, would get me nothing.

Scott Vogel, Watson and I got smashed in a bar. I was close to tears. Seeing my dream slowly dissolve was hard. Vogel was strong and supportive. He knew there had to be a solution.

I need to choose a DP for artistic merit, not for economics and convenience. I am now hoping that my great collaborator Matthew Libatique will be available. If he is, I will do everything to make it a reality.

AUGUST 12, 1.50PM: TESTS, ALLIES, ENEMIES

Finally, positivity: after a bit of soul-searching Matthew Libatique has agreed to shoot π. His music video career has just begun to take off and he's concerned that if he takes a break to shoot a movie he'll lose his place in line. I explained to him gently that he is a narrative film-maker

On the set of Euclid: Director of Photography Matthew Libatique (left) and 1st AC Chris Bierlein (right)

and videos are parasitic television commercials and quickly he jumped on board.

Matty is the right choice. He will make up for his lack of feature experience with passion and talent. He has an amazing eye and an amazing touch. He lights and operates. We have very similar taste because, like Eric and myself, he grew up with hip-hop culture in Queens. We also have a past.

Two years ago we spent a horrid month in the Philippines working together on an evil war movie. It was a vicious battle with no money and no artistic merit. But Matty was more than a trooper. Afterwards, we took the little money we had saved in the jungle and went to Thailand for New Year's. As midnight, December 31, 1994 rolled in, we were at a 72-hour rave on a beach on Ko Pha Ngan – an island off of southern Thailand. The tide came in, the sun came up, everyone kept dancing; the tide went out, the sun went down, everyone kept dancing. I was miserable because I wasn't making films. All I was doing was work for the Man. Matty cheered me up and told me it would happen. I'm not sure if I believed him. Matty was there.

Our production designer is a young guy named Matthew Maraffi. This is his first feature. Eric found him; he just came off the Broadway show *Rent*, which he art-directed. He seems down-to-earth and hardworking.

He's about to begin building Euclid, Max's homemade supercomputer. We've spent the last months collecting old computer junk and storing it in Sean's apartment on the Bowery. Yesterday, I recycled twenty monitors and seven modems from the trash outside a cop station. I hailed a cab. The cabbie was like, 'Really?' I was like, 'Yeah.' He shrugged, another crazy New Yorker playing with trash, as he popped the trunk. I shlepped everything over to Sean's place on the Bowery. His small bedroom is filling up with old computer hardware – it fits into his method, sleeping with the smell of silicon.

Sean Gullette in the lighting warehouse in Bushwick, Brooklyn, where Euclid was soon to be built. Lots of work to turn the tiny Mac Classic into a super computer.

Scott Vogel's father has a lighting factory in Bushwick, Brooklyn. We're going to build Euclid in the back room. It's a hell of a neighborhood, you pass by pit bulls and junkies if you take the subway. But it's free and the space is perfect.

AUGUST 26, 5.15PM: DEVIL'S CANDY

The almighty dollar is laughing scornfully in my face. My destiny is being held up by $17,000. Eric's destiny, Matty's, Sean's, Franklin's, Vogel's, Maraffi's, Oren's, all of us – for $17,000? What is $17,000? It's nothing, it's weak, it's empty, it's pathetic. I know that we will get the money and laugh at this one day, but it is so frustrating to be held up by chump change.

Otherwise things are so strong. Everything is brewing and everyone is juiced. Sean's work is intense. He's still pushing the emotions a bit too hard, but it's easy to bring

Sketch of Euclid by Matthew Maraffi

stuff down. The other way – pumping stuff up – is a problem. He nails the scenes and makes stellar choices. He knows the questions to ask and he follows the inner logic of the character through the scene as well as through the film. His questions continue to challenge me and they are constantly sending me back to the keyboard for a rewrite.

Sean focusing on his character between shots in the belly of Euclid.

This week is filled with:
1 chasing $.
2 callbacks.
3 getting Euclid built.

Euclid is going to be a great computer – a real character. We've already collected almost two tons of old computer and electronic parts. They will form the basis for Max's apartment. Maraffi's sketches evolve daily.

SEPTEMBER 13, 11AM: PIMPS AND HOS

To help raise the much-needed $, I turn to prostitution. This time it is truly the Man – a multi-billion-dollar oil company hired me to video an industrial that teaches people how to pump gas. Idiot company, idiot subject matter, idiot goal. But I did it for the quick fee which went directly into the meager holdings of Protozoa. Sean came along to grip for me and play a gas station attendant.

Associate producer Scott Franklin came up with 'The scheme to end all schemes'. Franklin is a tough Jew from Long Island. He flew out from LA to work on the movie and his no-shit-taking energy is great. At his suggestion, we've been asking every person we know for $100. We drew up a clever letter and searched our Rolodexes. The letter is doing well. People seem positive and ten have already come through. Anything to get it done.

SEPTEMBER 14, NOON: DEEP SEA FISHIN'

Abe Vigoda, aka Fish, aka Tessio, wanted to do the movie. I spent a week talking to him about it, but he wanted $15,000 for three days – absolutely ridiculous. We explained our finances and offered him a very generous $5,000. But he turned it down. Here's a real dramatic role, something he never sees nowadays, and he won't do it. Instead, he'll go on making $660/day on *Conan O'Brien*, wearing a blond wig and playing a clown.

SEPTEMBER 15, 5.30PM: MUSIQUE NON STOP

Very Good News: Clint Mansell from Pop Will Eat Itself wants to score the film. I like him. We hung out the other night and he was very insightful into the project. He's primarily an electronic musician, which intrigues me. Real electronic musicians are a lot like Max Cohen in that they're paranoid hermits who hide in their cubby holes with homemade computer systems looking for the soul in the machine. Also the contrast of the smooth electronica with the grainy, edgy feel of the black and white negative film will be a good marriage.

SiouxZ, our music supervisor, has done PR for everyone in the electronica world from Nine Inch Nails to Prodigy. Electronic music is on the cover of *Time* and I hope the buzz doesn't burn out before π is done. Now, all we need is a sound designer.

SiouxZ and Eric are leaning towards Brian Emrich, a bass player and member of Foetus. I went by his house and it was more like a museum. He has a studio out in Brooklyn filled with collectibles. His major collection is paperback pulp and it is remarkable. He has endless stacks and stacks of books in plastic bags. Everything is incredibly neat and organized. I like minds more obsessive than mine. He also told me that he's thinking of buying a mummy. A real mummy – a 2,000-year-old mummified woman. I hired him on the spot.

SEPTEMBER 24, 2.10PM: BEG BORROW STEAL

Franklin's $100 scheme is working pretty well. We've brought in over three grand. I'm hoping an executive producer is going to step in with some big $, and we're looking hard, sending our package out to everyone we can.

When I was picking up my last check from the Evil Petroleum Empire, I noticed a room filled with old computers and parts. I told them they could keep the $500 they still owed me if they let me empty their room. They were more than thrilled. I sent for Franklin and the van and we packed the shit out of it. I think we finally have enough raw material to build Euclid.

I am extremely nervous. I problem-solve twenty-four/seven. While I'm asleep my mind is firing questions, trying to figure out how I'm going to do a scene. How to raise the $. How I'm going to finish storyboarding. So much to do. Time is limited and I need to get into the flow.

I've been trying to convince some of my friends to stop shaving. I tell them if they grow beards I'll put them in the film. Only my neuro-scientist friend Ari Handel has agreed. So, I've decided to stop shaving in case we are short of extras for the Hasid scene. I hate acting, but I'll stand in the background if the camera needs it. The other pro-beard anti-shaving argument is that the facial growth is gonna put a few years on me and, hopefully, I'll get some more respect from the actors who are weary of young first-time directors. Nevertheless, all of these reasons are not gonna stop my mom from taunting me.

SEPTEMBER 27, 1AM: LIVING TRUTHFULLY UNDER IMAGINARY CIRCUMSTANCES

I'm supposed to be cast by tonight, but it didn't happen. I am very tired. *Very tired.* I can't wait to hit my bed and zonk out into nothingness. I spring for the $10 cab to Hell's Kitchen. On the radio is the Offspring, which brings back memories of LA. I must admit I have my doubts about π. Someone said a man without doubts is a man without widsom. But my doubts are due to my lack of skill and preparation. I know that with more time I could be ready, but now I am not ready. Too much to do. Too much. I need a Sol – the mentor, the glue, the human side of Max's life. I need a Sol badly!!!

Need sleep. Max = Sean. Lenny = Ben Shenkman. Rav Cohen = Stephen Pearlman. Marcy Dawson = Pamela Hart. Sol = ? Lotsa work.

OCTOBER 4, 1.24PM: THE GRANDMA BETTY SCENE

I called Grandma. She asked me where the movie was going to show. It was the first time I ever really spoke more than four lines of dialogue with her. Our script is always the same:

ME: Hi Grandma! It's me.
GRANDMA BETTY: Hi darling.
ME: How are you?
GRANDMA BETTY: OK, I've been a little sick.
ME: Are you feeling a little better?

GRANDMA BETTY: A little. I'll talk to you later.
ME: All right. I love you.
GRANDMA BETTY: I love you too.
Click.

The TV is always on in the background. Blaring. She always wants me to call, but she always wants to get off the phone.

So, we've pushed for one more week – largely because Sol was not cast.

OCTOBER 6, 9.30PM: SPIRALS EVERYWHERE

Drove Matty and Eric downtown and loaded the car up with stuff for a test in Brooklyn. We're going to shoot a new scene I've added in Coney Island. I think that after the second headache scene the audience needs a break

Guerilla film-making in Coney Island armed only with a reflector and a Bolex. From left to right: Darren Aronofsky, Matthew Libatique, Howard Simon, Matthew Maraffi, Lora Zuckerman and Sean Gullette.

and I think an organic, natural break will be strongest. Thus, Coney Island. It will allow me to show the spiral in the Nautilus shell.

Also, I can stick in my favorite character that I've ever written: King Neptune. African-spirited Rabbi Abe Levitsky will play the role. He is King Neptune deeply in soul and spirit. President of the Polar Bear Club of Coney Island and brother of handball legend Morris Levitsky, he is a true Brooklyn original. I met him seven years ago while filming a documentary in Brooklyn.

Neptune has lost his trident and so he's been using a metal detector to try to find it beneath the sand. When he finds it he'll regain his magic. But that doesn't mean he can't take a beat to appreciate a perfect spiral in one of his creations.

I remember in high school science learning about DNA and making the visual connection to the Milky Way. Sean thinks I'm a reductionist and doesn't buy into this spiral stuff. We argue, debate, sometimes scream – always with love. Personally, I don't think it's this end-all universal form connected to God. But I do think it's awfully strange that our smallest ingredient (DNA) and our largest macro-structure (the Milky Way) are so similar in shape.

OCTOBER 7, 11PM: MEETING THE MENTOR

Two actors come in for Sol. Denise Fitzgerald, our casting director, is casting *Home Alone 3* and doesn't join us. Am I upset? What do you think? First actor is a soap star named Gil Rogers. OK actor but not right.

Next is Mark Margolis. All we know about him is that he was Antonio, the bomb maker, in *Scarface*. Very, very strong actor – an Actor's Studio veteran. I tell him not to worry about the Russian accent. Countless actors who have read for Sol have come in and tried the accent and sounded like complete morons. Mark tells me not to worry about the accent and dives into it. He's amazing. His accent is dead on. The other Sols we've read with are all charming and kindly and grandfatherly. With Margolis, you can see Sol's prison time, his cynicism, his bitterness, as well as his concern for Max. He's brilliant – completely against type for the role, which gives it another dimension. Is this Sol?

OCTOBER 8, MIDNIGHT: SEX AND VIOLENCE

Samia Shoaib and Ajay Naidu and Clint meet me at my sister's. Clint is gonna help me record Samia and Ajay's sex and violence scenes that Max hears through the walls. The violence is weak but the sex is steamy.

Later, me and Clint ride down to the office and we have a nice chat about him being a rock star. I ask him what it's like to rock out 20,000 people. He answers simply in his Brit accent, 'It's fucking greet!' Maybe I should have been a musician.

Then, I find the office kicking and Denise flipping. She is pissed! Seems Sean called to inspire her to get us a good Sol. Sean was trying to be helpful and throw her some good energy. She flips, wondering if we question her commitment. I think about *Home Alone 3*, but I don't say it. I calm her down and tell her I want Mark Margolis. She's fine fifteen minutes later. For weeks she's been questioning our choice of Sean, which infuriates me, but I let it go because our casting director problem is . . . problematic.

We originally chose a casting director who almost destroyed the film. He offended countless agents and managers and many of them turned against the project. It caused us ridiculous problems. We had to serve him a cease-and-desist letter when an actor threatened to complain to SAG about him. Truly a nightmare. As soon as we fired him, I started looking for a casting director and

Denise fitted the bill. She came in last minute and it was a very brave thing to do. She wrote a bunch of letters to all the agents and managers telling them that casting π was her baby now. I am very grateful.

OCTOBER 9, 10.29PM: ROLLING THE DICE

Coney Island dailies look like *shit*. Matty and I are very upset. The blacks are gray and the whites are gray. We need to do something radical. Negative film sucks and we discuss the possibility of reversal. It's a very risky thing to do for many reasons. First, it's very expensive. Second, it's very hard to negative cut. Third, there's no latitude: you *have* to nail the exposure.

On the other hand, the results with reversal can be startlingly stark and high contrast. The film could look great. Matty tells me he wants to concentrate on exposure, and he feels up to the challenge. I'm very nervous, but I agree. I don't want a gray film. I want something that's super contrasty and very challenging and new to audiences.

Eric is going to the Brooklyn Go Club, and I'm going to stretch and then hang with Dan Getz, our talented and affordable attorney. Met him through my parents, who met his parents on a cruise in the Caribbean. Like everyone on this film, he's a rookie.

OCTOBER 10, 8.43PM: NOT FUCKING FUNNY

We shoot in five days. I get a call from Sean. He sounds completely messed up, slurring: he tells me he's in Providence, Rhode Island, and says he thinks his leg is broken. I take a deep breath to not flip out before I realize he's just at a pay phone in New York, fucking with me. A little humor to release pre-shoot jitters.

Let me tell you, there's a lot of fear in making a movie, when you invest everything you have – money, friendships, your reputation – into a project. I realize that you must not think about what might happen with the film. Don't count your chickens, etc. Bottom line is you don't know what you have until you have it. So the secret is to go out and make it.

Oren Sarch is our editor and I'm excited to have him. He's got a great sense of rhythm and style and he's very dedicated to the process. He's been at every pre-production meeting. He's growing a beard so he can be a Hasid extra in the shul scene.

OK, good news, finally. It looked like we were going to lose our last shot at the thirty Gs, but things turned around and it now looks like two investors Randy Simon and David Godbout, with the help of my friend Scott Silver, may come through.

The night before we begin, I am on the phone begging for money. I'd rather be in bed or with my notes, but I have got to work ol' pimp daddy for the cash and the car keys. Damn, this money thing sucks. I gave away the ship. We, the film-makers, are in some ways being sucked dry but I hope the experience of making the film will make up for all the financial pain.

Casting is done. Went with Mark Margolis and Sean to Go Club last night. It was very interesting. We learned a lot. Sean ate a ham sandwich. Then, there was our launch party at Truth and Soul, our production office. Everyone is cool. We have a good, young crew and everyone is juiced. Tom Tumminello showed up and he will be an excellent Ephraim.

We're psyched. Nothing else really, except we're on the

verge of filming. Sean threw up last night at 4.30am. Ham or nerves? We're all set. Everyone is up for it. Let's go.

PRODUCTION: THE SHOOT BEGINS

OCTOBER 14, 9.19PM: APPROACHING THE INMOST CAVE

It all starts at 6.45 this morning with the circle. The entire crew and cast joined hands and we all formed an economic and artistic partnership, a socialist collective. I made a speech from my heart. I thanked all and offered everyone a chance to take risks, a chance to make π their own, a chance at a meaningful collaboration. I almost cried. My mom did. (She's doing craft services.) Now we shoot – no more excuses.

This is really my first artistic move that is honest and separate from all those evil outside forces that twist and corrupt you. I must seize it.

Eric and I have decided to put our commie leanings to the test. Fifty percent of the film's profits will go to our investors. The other fifty percent will be divided equally amongst all the film-makers. What this means is that Eric, Sean and myself will profit equally alongside the production assistants, DP, loader, gaffer, etc.

In return, we hope that the crew and cast will make this film their own.

OCTOBER 17, 11.47PM: NO SLEEP TILL BROOKLYN

Day 4. Very tired – so I'll just write in notes:

OK, I've shot 6,200 feet.

Did cool shot over on Ming Mecca. Camera was on a ladder looking upon the entire set. Euclid is beautiful. Maraffi and Sean did a great job. It is alive.

The Ming Mecca chip looks like the black box of a tefillin.

Dad on set, I think he was impressed.

Had to change Euclid's 'mainframe chip', which we did, a good last-minute choice. Cost us time, but it looked damn good. Had a small fight with Maraffi when I critiqued his original chip. I wanted something much simpler. Ralph, who works at the lighting factory, cut six square pieces of chips on his table saw and Matty and I glue-gunned them together in five minutes. Maraffi felt sorry afterwards. Everyone is passionate and the crew is driven.

We move slow but shit looks great.

We are going to lose Ariyela (our Israeli make-up artist) for the last week of the shoot. Too bad, I like her. And her training with Israeli secret services makes her a great film-maker.

Ride to Brooklyn every morning, pre-dawn, is long and hard, dark and tired. Pick up Sean on the corner of Bowery and Delancey, a block from his house. He's wearing Max's clothes and I think he's starting to forget who he is. He's quiet and focused. Doesn't talk to the crew. Doesn't laugh. Good, very good. Inspirational for us all.

Mornings I'm depressed, but nights are juicy but exhausted.

OCTOBER 20, 11.45PM: THE FACTORY

The factory has a huge sliding front door and a hangar-like work area, where Ralph is making lamps all day long, operating a range of noisy heavy machinery. When we need custom lights, Ralph can build them on the spot.

My mom and her best friend Jo Gordon have taken over the old kitchen. They've cleaned everything up and serve three meals a day. Lunch and dinner come from Mendy's, the Kosher Sports bar where Izzi has a barter arrangement. She has bagels and juice and Coke all day. Jo plays her acoustic guitar and prepares herself for the roll of the Evil Landlady, Mrs Ovadia.

Craft services: Jo Ovadia (left) and Charlotte Aronofsky (right)

It's nice to have two mother figures on set. The rest of the crew are film kids from NYU, so my mom and Jo add a maturity to the set. I know eventually we'll all melt down into insanity, but they definitely introduce a counterpoint. Also, no one makes a better peanut butter and jelly sandwich than my mom.

Izzi the Barter King was discovered by Eric and me while casting for real Hasids. It turns out that he's the president of HAG, the Hasidic Actors Guild. Their motto is pay us for *pais*. This is all in jest, but the self-declared Kosher-Ham loves being in movies and for a role in the film and some back-end he's secured us our first week of food.

When Eric is on set, he has the mobile production office on a craft services table by the kitchens, with a Powerbook, a phone, and plastic files. We have taken seats out of the van as couches. There are two small bathrooms for a crew, on average, of twenty-two people.

At the center of the building is a forty-foot-high storage barn, with skylights and rusty tin plates overhead. Next to

The iodine scene. Devi (Samia Shoaib)
and Max (Sean Gullette)

this is a courtyard and sealed-off alley which Sean has
made into his holding area. He spends his down time
alone, pacing around, smoking too many cigarettes and
doing push-ups. When he's not on set, Sean is always
preparing psychologically for the next take. Sometimes he
forgets to switch off his wireless mic and Ken Ishii, the
sound man, records him talking to himself or taking a piss.

We have a Go board made of cardboard and black tape,
with a bunch of bolts spray-painted black and white for
pieces. Everyone has learned or is learning how to play, so
now there are Go games whenever we have a break. At
lunch people spread out, sitting on the concrete floor, and
eat all over the building. We have to police our crumbs or
the big rats will come out. My mom seals up everything at
night, but even so, they made their way through three
layers of plastic. Aggressive fucking rats in Bushwick.

Electricity comes from a huge, ancient box out of a
Terry Gilliam movie, which our vegan gaffer Sinclair

Smith has tapped and cabled up to the set. Max's apartment is up a rickety flight of metal stairs. Windows taped over and sealed shut – like he would have them – also means no worries about daylight bleeding in. Two of the walls will retract for certain shots. Behind one of them is the make-up chair and Ariyela's area. Computer stuff everywhere, a desk, a bed, a chair, a phone, a bathroom. Inside it feels and smells lived-in and authentic. Even the lighting cables and Maraffi's tools blend into the forest of computer cables. Very tight quarters, and hot when the lights are going, but it feels right.

OCTOBER 21, 11.21PM: THE HURRICANE

Week one ended hard. We did Max's hallway in Jo Gordon's building. We didn't have landlord's permission, and it gave everything an edge. Either way, the landlords are Hasidic and we were filming on a Saturday, so we didn't have much interaction with them. There was a vicious hurricane outside and it rained out the first game of the World Series, Yanks vs. Braves. I'm glad the series is on, but I don't want it to become a distraction. The Yankees getting their asses kicked means less baseball interest from the crew – more focus on π.

The day was almost twenty hours – all of the landlady, indoor Jenna and Samia in the hallway stuff, plus the staircase. Hard. Matty had a vicious headache attack. But he stuck in there. He had the wrong lens for the peep-hole shots – Max's POV through the door. I told him several times to get a wider lens, but he dropped the ball. I got pissed and it ended up eating up our time.

After wrap I had my ceremonial cigarette and then I got a beer alone at Captain Walters, a couzine bar in Sheepshead Bay. My mind was racing with the compromises I had to make. Film is all about compromises. It's impossible to get everything you want:

weighing the time we can afford against what is important to get and what will hurt the film if we don't get.

Today started well, but we really slowed down in the afternoon. After lunch is always a bitch. No dailies yet. Haven't seen a single frame of exposed film.

OCTOBER 22, 11.33PM: CRANKY

Day 8 started off pissy. Matty screamed at Lora, the first AD, and then he asked me to talk to him directly instead of through Lora. I agree with this and must follow this new protocol. Then I exploded on Maraffi. Maraffi stormed off set and apparently barfed because he was sick. I apologized. And now Ariyela is gonna be pissed when she realizes I did the blood for Max's nose myself when she was off set.

Cool opening shot to the film, though: roll from out-of-focus into focus on Max passed out on his desk with a nosebleed.

Gotta save film. We shot inserts today. High contrast means we need many close-ups. Cut the masters. Go for close-ups.

At the end of the day, we all watched dailies for the first time. We went up to Max's apartment and played the tape over the VCRs we have hooked up for the computer monitors. Must say they looked really contrasty. This film definitely looks unlike any feature I've ever seen. It is really wild. Pure blacks and pure whites, and many of the images look like beautiful stills. I know now how to look at the images I see in the viewfinder and our little video-tape monitor. I think some of the crew were a little shocked at how extreme the look is. Sean has decided not to look at any dailies – which I approve of – and he said the crew seemed very subdued when they came out.

Either way, I've shot 14,000 feet, which is two-fifths of my entire load. It's a bit scary. The ratio will drop for dialogue coverage. It has to.

NOVEMBER 2, 12.22PM: THE IMPORTANCE OF DOING HOMEWORK

We looked at the second batch of dailies last night. Matty hit the exposure on almost everything. Still a few problems, but nothing we cannot overcome. It made us feel good.

Today is Scott Vogel's wedding, but Director, DP, Producer and AD need to work on shot list. Five or six of us are living at my and Eric's 600-square-foot apartment. Matty and his wife in the claustrophobic loft. Lora on the dirty couch. The occasional friend or grip on the floor. And the vampire in Eric's room. It makes focusing a challenge. But nothing is as important as homework.

NOVEMBER 6, 1.30AM: HELL

Today was the worst day of shooting, as well as one of the worst days of my life. It started with Headache 3 – a stunt-intensive scene – and we were unprepared. Everything is going slow or wrong. At one point Sean is supposed to break the mirror with his head. I know he is ready to do it right now, but Ariyela insists that we cover the mirror with Plexiglass to avoid glass splinters. Maraffi finds a piece of Plexi, but it is so thick that during the take the mirror won't break, and Sean smashes it with his fist in frustration.

Maraffi tells me he's got a new job starting tomorrow. Shit is pent up. Then, there's Sean's performance. I'd love to attach all the negativity to Sean's outstanding work, but truly it would be a lie. I was ill-prepared. My fault.

Nonetheless, Sean was amazing. Absolutely overwhelming.

Later, outside I started to heave and barf and sob and pass out. I begged for life, the film, everything to end. I was dying. My heart was super fast, my mind cluttered. I don't know why – overload. I was fed up and the anger was pent up. I was lost and confused and depressed.

Eric told me – as I lay in child's pose in the dark nighttime courtyard – 'You have one choice . . . persevere.' 'Or,' I replied, 'I could drive off the bridge.' 'No, you can't,' Eric answers, 'or I would have done that a week ago.' Got to remember the beauty of what we're doing. Remember Joanne's face when we wrapped her. She glowed.

Sixteen hours after we started, we got most of the day. I'm behind a few tight shots. Hard stuff. Hard stuff *mañana*. But it will be better.

NOVEMBER 7, 1.07AM: HEAVEN

What a day. The shul. Incredible location and great energy. Stephen Pearlman was amazing. The beard was great, but the angles are slightly comical and I'm worried that the scene may be laughed at. Fingers crossed that it plays dark. The film is so dark already, I hope it will hold.

Darren directs Henri Falconi while Stephen Pearlman
(center) watches

The rabbi who runs the shul, Ari Handel, and Oren were extras. At lunchtime, Ariyela shaved Sean's head, and Eric got his head shaved in solidarity.

Sean did amazingly different things with each take. He experimented and I know we got it.

NOVEMBER 8, 11.20PM: ROLL 100

Mark Margolis and Sol 4 and 5. Lauren Fox. Took a long time to get the performances out of Mark. He was resisting and I knew why. The scene was poorly written and Mark knew it. But this wasn't the time to repair it. In the end I got the anger and rage out of him. It was good. Margolis cracks jokes until I say action and then he is right in it.

But everyone was tired, and we had a very late start. Somehow, we shot roll 100 and the generous David Godbout bought us champagne.

One more week. Ariyela is on for the whole shoot. Her other film was pushed, a relief. When we wrapped out of

Sol (Mark Margolis) pleads with Max

Sol's we caught the last out of the World Series. The Yankees won and as we drove home we joined the spontaneous street fiestas.

NOVEMBER 9, 12.22PM: CHINESE CHAMPAGNE

We waited for hours at Truth and Soul and finally the daily tapes came. Jonah, the best boy, the second AC, a bunch of grips, Matty and I watched dailies. It was a real bonding experience, because the footage was awesome. Matty was very happy. There were many compromises, but the footage is working. It's alive on the screen. We drank champagne and ate Chinese.

NOVEMBER 10, NOON: EXTREME CLOSE-UP

Today was pick-ups. Lots of them: 182 takes, 58 set-ups. Amazing big day. Lots of cool stuff. We shot tons of Max's point of view. The camera was over his shoulder the entire time and it was very difficult tight work for him.

Matty is supposed to leave on Saturday. I hope he will stay longer. We'll shoot some Oxberry stuff, I hope.

Sean continues to give one hundred percent. He is the man.

NOVEMBER 11, 5.11AM: THE SUPREME ORDEAL

One of our longest days just ended. Day started Sunday at 8am, it is now Monday morning. That makes it twenty-one hours and the entire crew ain't in bed yet. Eric leaned hard on me for going late, but it is the last week and now is not the time to compromise.

Max destroyed Euclid tonight. Shot it in a wide shot from above to be safe and it looked a bit weak, but the flashes really helped. All of Chris Bierlein's technology and expertise has been extremely helpful. Maraffi was emotional – his baby, hundreds of hours of work destroyed, totalled, dead. I reminded him that it will always be remembered on celluloid.

Sean and I had friction. I did not pay enough respect to his headache at the head of the Euclid destruction shot. He jumped on me and was pissed off for most of the day, which was a very important one. But I managed to use that energy somehow. Hours later, at 3am, with the HMI light pouring in the window and everyone exhausted and red-eyed, we had to shoot the Devi scene, part of the climax of the film. Very delicate emotionally, and I knew I had to bring him down. The scene needed it. But Sean was all over the place and fighting me. We were both tired and wired and he wasn't trusting me. I told him to stop fighting me, but he wouldn't. Then I told him that we had the same intentions – to make a great film – and that for that to happen he needed to trust me. The whole crew standing around in silence. He finally calmed down. I had him take several breaths and then right before we filmed, I had him hug Samia. Five minutes later, I let the sound roll, then the camera, then hit the slate, then I called for places. And then action . . . nice take.

NOVEMBER 12, 2.52AM: PURPLE HEART

Started the day with the closing scene of the film, in the park with Jenna. Kristyn and Sean jammed the scene and I think it'll be awesome. Max's closing emotion is very hard to articulate and express – some type of existential acceptance of *now* – but Sean nailed it.

Talked to Oren and he said some of the overexposed is unusable. It's very upsetting and I hope it doesn't damage the film. I have a feeling it might cut anyway. We will see.

Late night in midtown, very cold. Matty took a big spill and it was very scary. During the Marcy Dawson chase, one of the tough guys Peter Cheyenne, a bit over-aggressive, knocked him over as he was running full-speed with the Aaton under his arm. Matty landed on his knees, stayed down, and started shaking. He wasn't responding – we're thinking, he's in shock. I stepped in, people went running for a hospital, a cop showed up, and then a strange thing happened. Dave, who was playing the other tough guy, bent over Matty and started talking to him. I began to stop him, but Peter told me that Dave was a coach. Dave told Matty to get up and get off his butt. He was very aggressive, but Matty responded. We got Matty up and sent him off to Scott Vogel's to rest. Matty was just bruised and scraped – tired, cold and frustrated, and in some pain. He was more worried about the camera than his knees. Both were OK.

We packed in and had to skip the footbridge scene, but we'll grab it on Friday.

NOVEMBER 13, 1.13AM: VIVA LAS VEGAS

Strange dream last night: I was in Vegas with someone who reminded me half of Eric and half of a debonair Sean. We were dressed to the nines. On the back of a Vespa, the Eric/Sean character had a beautiful model whom we took to wine and dine. For this part of the dream I was a background character, almost a ghost. At some fancy hotel restaurant we ordered steaks and started eating. The Eric/Sean character confessed that he had no money and nowhere to stay.

I realized that there was a girl watching me. It turned out to be a pretty girl named Tara whom I knew in high school. We caught up and tried to make plans for later. I went to borrow Eric/Sean's beeper, but he didn't have it. The piece of steak I was chewing stuck in my mouth like dry chalk. Finally, I swallowed it and got her address which was a villa in the mock Italy section of this hotel, right above the catacombs. I asked if they had a minotaur character with an axe, and Tara and her mom replied that they weren't sure: they hadn't been on the ride.

Then, there was arguing and I realized it was my dad and mom fighting with someone. I turned around and slowly the room became my Uncle Barney's apartment on Pembroke Street in Brooklyn. Barney was lying in bed like the dying old guy in *Titticut Follies*. Mom and Dad were screaming at him to let us film the White Void scene on his bed. I told them that we don't need to. I was short and to the point. Then Barney sat up, he seemed healthy and rosy. He didn't recognize me because of my new-grown beard, but then he said it looked good. I awoke wondering about Barney's health.

No one had a clue what it meant. Then, King John Ta – our second assistant camera – shared his dream. He dreamt that we were on location at a giant spiral staircase. He lugged all the equipment to the top where there was a giant chandelier. Scott Franklin was hanging on the light and Lora was screaming at him to get down. Everyone laughed, probably because it wasn't too different from reality.

Then, our key grip, Trevor, shared his latest conspiracy dream. He dreamt that Max was on the subway watching the different numbered trains pull in and out of the station. First went the three, then the one, then the four . . .

We've all become part of the film. Our minds have been invaded. We're all exhausted. We let Ta and Trevor leave early. They need their pillows.

NOVEMBER 14, 6.30AM: SURVIVAL OF THE FITTEST

All-nighter. Went pretty well. The gun and Marcy's desperation will hopefully not be over the top. Pam was real good; she nailed it. I made a mistake by making her first shot the difficult one including the speech. It threw her off, and she told me how hard it was for her to jump right in it. She was really out of energy, but she summoned a lot from somewhere and really did some very nice stuff. It was freezing cold, but somehow she performed. At one point I was terrified because her skin was actually blue.

Something about the chase scene night: I operated the camera for most of the night, except the sequence when Matty fell, and I realized in order to do that you must be very rehearsed. It's so fucking hard to focus on four actors, frame and light all at once. One actor, no moves, I can handle, but moving all around was hard and I'm sure my hesitation will show.

We shot Max hiding under the car with a wide 5.9 lens and it was cool. I love lying on my belly in the gutter making movies. Hardcore guerrilla style.

NOVEMBER 15, 10.22PM: REWARD (SEIZING THE SWORD)

Last night of principal photography. Just got into bed. Very tired. Nearly fell asleep in the car after dropping off Sean, Ben and Tom Tumminello. Tom offered to be dropped off at a train, but I would have hated myself later. He gave so much to Ephraim, really believed in it.

Good mood on set. Mom and Jo wrapped and hugged everyone goodbye. Dad was happy to be around. No circle – we'll wait until the wrap party.

Car scene, kind of good; good performances, I think. Either that or I'm totally off. Izzi brought his station wagon and drove like a madman on acid. We filmed until dawn reached the Brooklyn heavens. Will we go to Sundance and recognition?

NOVEMBER 27, 12.41PM: W-R-A-P

Wrapped for real. Wow. Matty, Lora and I were up all night at our apartment in Hell's Kitchen. Filming a tiny area with a macro lens. Fun stuff: just the camera and lots of details. Matty and I had a grand time trading shots and going crazy. Sean slept in Eric's room while we were set up in the living room. Every once in a while we'd wake him up for a shot and then he'd go back and fall down.

Then I went to sleep. I was too exhausted to write in the journal.

Sunday we did Snorri Cam and 12fps point-of-view stuff of Chinatown. Fun with me and Matty. Sean got into working in the rig – running down Canal Street full-tilt with me and Matty spotting the camera.

Sunday night: big night – wrap party at the Fez, very fun. David and Randy were very generous. I shaved my beard and put on a suit; no one in the crew recognized me. Lotsa drinks.

Then we did the circle. I had everybody grab hands. I talked about the war we just fought and I thanked everyone and once again I almost cried. My mom did. It was a great, hard, vicious journey. Joanne wrote a song about our times

The Snorri-Cam is propped for Max's destruction of the brain. 1st AC Chris Bierlein

and tribulations on set, to the melody of 'Thanks for the Memory', and we all sang the chorus together. Acoustic guitar and all. Pam Hart really got into it.

We find out that *Filmmaker* magazine has done a production update column on us. Thank you, Mary Glucksman. She wrote a good thousand words on us for the Sundance issue. Very good placement. Just stumbled on this:

> Maybe *all* systems – that is, any theoretical, verbal, symbiotic, semantic, etc., formulation that attempts to act as an all-encompassing, all-explaining hypothesis of what the universe is about – are the manifestations of paranoia. We should be content with the mysterious, the meaningless, the contradictory, the hostile, and most of all the unexplainably warm and giving.

> Philip K. Dick
> Vancouver SF Convention, 1972

That pretty much sums up π.

POST-PRODUCTION

DECEMBER 26, 2.45PM: CALIFORNIA HERE I COME

Christmas in LA. I should know better.

Went to dinner at casting director Mary Vernieu's house in Venice. I've wanted to meet her for quite a while. Hang out with film-makers Marc Waters, Scott Silver and Beau Flynn.

I came out here on the eighteenth to house-sit, catch up with some people, and to work on some new stories. Very challenging to get back into the writing phase. My post-shoot hangover is slowly fading. Artist Ed Flynn gave me a bunch of the drawings for π, *The Book of Ants*, our comic-book version of the film. They are beautiful.

New Year's Eve in LA. I should know better.

I'm going to Trevor Groth's party tonight. He's a cool guy who works at Sundance. A real film-lover, with style and good taste, probably the man most likely to get π.

Things are rough with the film. The stuff looks great, but I found out that we have a twelve grand bill at Bono, our lab. This figure easily puts the budget somewhere at 25–45 percent over. We need to go out there and *beg* for some cash, otherwise it is over. I can't let this happen to my family, friends and actors who are involved in this film – we have to get Post moving. But it's not going to be easy.

FEBRUARY 14, 1997, MIDNIGHT: THE ROAD BACK

Valentine's Day back in NYC. Two days after my birthday. I'm twenty-eight years old. The assemblage is almost cut. Hubert Selby's *The Room* haunts me. The images and concepts in the book disturb me so much that I'm embarrassed to read it in public. Even on the subway, where you can do anything.

Staying at my sister's while she's off in North Carolina doing a story for CBS News. I bought a lucite Frank Lloyd Wright-style doll's house for her and I'm hoping it will blow her mind.

I slept late on my b-day. I went out to eat with the parents at Union Square Café. At night everyone met me at Mike's Bar and Grill. Present were: Dan Schrecker, Ari Handel, Sean Gullette, Amy Silver, Lucas Sussman, Kelly Stevens, Sue Johnson, Darcy T., Alexis Stern, Oren and his wife Gagan, Eric Cohen and his date Jennifer, Dan Getz, Kofi Ingersol, Colson Whitehead, and a few other cats. We proceed to get smashed on margaritas. Fun fun fun.

Some late night birthday thoughts: When you die, it's

43

not you walking around heaven or hell drinking champagne and trading one-liners with Abe Lincoln. Rather, the 'you' ceases to exist. Your ego goes bye-bye, but the energy that makes up you rejoins the pool of consciousness which forms everything. I think birth is the act of forgetting that we are all part of the same force. Birth is God sprouting eyes to stare at God. These eyes must *not know* that they are staring at God – which is themselves – because then they could not appreciate the beauty of their own existence. Birth is forgetfulness. Birth is the creation of ego, of self, of separation.

Tequila is good shit.

FEBRUARY 20, 6.05AM: REQUIEM

Palestrini is on the twenty-ninth floor, with a great view of midtown, a giant TV in the lounge and free drinks in the fridge. Working here I can almost forget how broke we are. The people who run it are starting to like π again – Oren has told them about our progress.

Clint and SiouxZ are now watching the assemblage, which I watched with Eric and Oren on Sunday. 133 minutes and 3.5 seconds. Quite an event. I think the film is somewhere in there, like Max's data.

I'm working on a haunted submarine movie with my college room-mate Lucas Sussman. We came up with the idea after watching Nicolas Roeg's *Walkabout*. Is it connected? No. It's just that good film gets the mind clicking.

My lawyer Andrew Hurwitz made an offer to Hubert Selby's agent, Stu Robinson at Paradigm, for *Requiem for a Dream*. I've been breaking down the book and am excited.

FEBRUARY 26, 3.47AM: CUTTING . . .

It seems that an assemblage exists. Sean came by to see it; he was quiet at first, but then began really to like it.

We need to cut on Sundays, so we may bring in an assistant. If we work eight to fifteen hours during the weekend, we're in the thirty-hour range, which is respectable, but gives me time to think.

Sleater-Kinney can have my soul, my body, my spirit, my dedication. Everything. I love that fucking band.

APRIL 7, 4.32PM: AND CUTTING . . .

Oren's office is becoming an existential purgatory and I am sinking deeper and deeper into his leather couch. Today is almost summer, hot. Editing is real slow. We are only up to Scene 20 of my cut. We *must* get an assistant to speed up the process.

I saw Al Pacino in *The Godfather* last night. The guy is so fucking amazing. Absolutely wonderful. I cried during the opening shot: 'I believe in America . . .' It wasn't just the performance, it was the film-making. Perfect, absolutely incredible, inspirational work.

Call Sean. We've begun writing the voice-over together. Our idea is to write it in the form of a lab report/personal journal.

Jeremy Dawson, one of my tight friends from college, has started working on titles. I told him that if they're good, I'll stick them on the front of the movie, otherwise we roll them at the end. We're doing them all computer-based on a Mac; it should keep costs down and creative possibilities vast. Eric has a great math book he should scan and steal images from. The era of visual sampling has begun.

Jeremy is a Renaissance man for the digital age. He can shoot pictures, he can shoot film, he teaches Photoshop, he can animate, he can write HTML, he learns any technical process overnight, he has superb taste, he can do anything. He's also a top-notch professional. If he says he'll do something, he does it.

Eight days until May 1, so I awoke at 8am after a four-hour sleep, sat up in bed, and called Oren to declare we are on emergency status. We need to finish the first cut by May 1, otherwise we are in trouble. We won't make the Toronto Film Festival deadline. Out of my window in Hell's Kitchen are little tweety birds and fluffy clouds. Little time to enjoy it.

Peter Broderick of the IFC saw the trailer and read our press and is very interested in the film. He wants to see an assemblage. The IFC has a finishing fund, and the fifty Gs we need isn't much for them.

Randy Simon has agreed to pay for our overages, which comes to $3,000 without the Bono bill. That's $1,000 for Palestrini, $1,000 for Vogel's dad's electric bill, $500 for Denise Fitzgerald and $500 for me to shoot some time-lapse shots.

Sleater-Kinney rules my life. *Call the Doctor* is a sick album.

A woman from Revolution Records has expressed strong interest in distributing the soundtrack. Ninety percent of the musicians we have contacted have agreed to participate in our soundtrack.

Clint and SiouxZ are spinning tonight at Otis, a bar in Hell's Kitchen. I will definitely go. In the basement of a thrift store, I found a bunch of medical gynecology books from before the 1920s and I knew that Brian Emerich (Sound Designer) would be interested: he's a sick fuck but very aware of it. Immaculate taste, the kid has. I know his sound work will be great.

We must decide what to do with the Plantain guys. They offered us $10,000, plus unlimited editing, for a 'Produced in Association with' credit. I need an answer from David and Randy. I'd love to get Plantain involved.

We're in bizness with Plantain. They're going to give us ten Gs *mañana* and we have ten weeks of time on their Avids. Tyler Brodie and Jonah Smith, very good people, are hard at work on their dream of creating the next Good Machine or Shooting Gallery, a full-range film production company, plus a record label. Work is finishing on their HQ in a converted parking garage. We have a bet to see who finishes first, Plantain or π. The space is going to be beautiful: recording studio, Avid bays, giant screening-room/shooting space with a catwalk, a big open office/kitchen/conference room. The aesthetic is sort of postmodern shantytown.

For now, I'm all alone, working days in a forest-green room in the basement of Tyler's house. I am slow, but I like cutting. I love the Avid. It's word processing with images.

It's going to be a hot and sweaty summer.

MAY 22, 8.50PM: FLOW

OK. We are cooking. Eric feels it too. Cutting so that days are forgotten. Always thinking about how to conquer the film. How to understand it and edit it and make it better.

Good note: If you don't want to face something in editing you needn't, as long as you move on and face something else with courage and direction. A feature is so large that you can leave something and return to revisit it. It's sort've like a Go game. The board is so complex and so many battles are waging that you can flow your attention from location to location. Just try to maintain a macro, larger vision of the entire piece and the honesty to answer to yourself if each micro moment is working.

Worked on the voice-over with Sean in the recording booth. Very hard stuff to get right, but we made good progress, came up with some good stuff. Sean was hard to work with at times, but ultimately it is me. I get frustrated, and I need to have patience and to relax. It is a very meticulous process, post-production, and you need to settle in and work at it. After Sean left, I spent the rest of the day logging his stuff.

Oren is going out to a concert. I hope we make our deadline.

JUNE 9, 11.43PM: OVERTURE

Horrible day at Plantain. One of their drives was faulty and it crashed with about 1,500 media files on it, which means all of last week's digitizing work is destroyed.

The biggest problem is the Toronto deadline. I am extremely stressed out, but I am trying to deal. Two beers from the fridge at Palestrini helped. Oren was tired, but we still got shit done.

And then Clint came up and gave me the opening title score, which is super dope. Sci-fi horror shit. Real cool. We'll lay it in *mañana*.

When you're working hard, creativity sparks one's skull. I am lovely with life, and ideas are pouring in by the millions. It is a great feeling, but it is hard to write them all down quick enough. It's an amazing rush.

Met with Lucas and pumped him up with horror stuff for the sub-script. We're calling it 'Critical Mass'.

JUNE 11, 1.22PM: BLOODY NOSES

My nosebleeds have started up again. A nosebleed was the second image of π. The first image was Sean digging into his head with an X-Acto blade. Edited the Snorri Cam Chinatown wandering scenes. I went a little crazy with them and I'm hoping they're not too wacked out.

How many people helped us on this film? How many names are going to be in the credits? 250? 300? There's the eighty people who gave us $100. There's got to be 400 names in the credits. Amazing.

Had lunch with Clint. Nervous guy. He was sure I hated his music because I didn't leave a positive message on the phone. We had a real bond today. We talked about our personal manic-depression trips. He told me he's been a bit gloomy of late, but that he's coming out of it. He's real excited about the film. His music is fantastic and it's going to really improve the film.

I know we will get the $37,000 to finish this. It is bigger than us now.

Black and white film is the way to learn. It's the way to figure out the world.

JUNE 12, 3.11PM: BREATHE

Tatjana is digitizing at Plantain. Oren is sick. I'm going to go to yoga and breathe. Nuff said.

JUNE 25, 8.28PM: THE FAT-TRIMMER

We missed Toronto. It's OK, though. The deadline pushed us to race to this point. Lotsa work has gotten done. Now, it's Park City, Utah, or bust.

Had our first screening with Dan Schrecker, Dan Cogan, Dave Shiskel, Mark Grant, Alan Zelnitz. My feeling is that they all felt it lagged and that the voice-over was way too much. All valuable information. I want to shave a good ten minutes out of the film.

Eighty minutes is a sexy number. It's long enough to be distributed as a feature in America and you also get an extra screening a day. I can't stand the latest two-hour trend in movies. Some movies need the time, but most drag. I want my plot and fireworks delivered quickly with no down time. I want roller-coaster rides not Ferris wheels. I want my MTV.

In the daytime I go to Plantain and cut by myself. Talked to Samia on the phone. We'll have a reshoot with her on Monday: just shoot her mouth saying, 'Max.' This will be a fantasy that will express Max's desire for her. I keep hearing that Max is hard to get to know, 'cause he is so emotionless. We may care for him more if he has desires – he longs for Devi. That will make him more alive.

This week I've been shaving, I am the fat-trimmer, the butcher boy. I've cut about two minutes out of the first forty-four scenes. We will see where this all goes.

My nosebleeds are vicious and they don't seem to be slowing down. The blood is endless.

JUNE 26, 1.08PM: SOMETIMES YOU GOTTA JUST GO SEE A MOVIE

It is the afternoon on a Sunday and I just got up. I gave the editing crew the weekend off. After a fantastic push the crew has earned it. Oren has probably seen more of my face and Sean's than his wife's in the months since he got married. We're all a bit exhausted and the break is exactly what I needed. I wish I had enough *dinero* to get out of town, but instead I went to see Kustarica's *Underground*, which was fair. Today I will go see Woo's *Face-Off* and hopefully have a nice time. I am broke.

One of the rolls from our reshoot came out black. All black. We do not know why. *Mañana* we do some more reshoots. I will shoot Samia.

I'm taking an acting class on Broadway. The teacher has a long history of teaching Sanford Meisner. Most of the students are stand-up comics who want to improve their acting work. Personally, I don't think I'll ever want to go in front of the camera. I just want to learn some techniques so that I can work better with actors.

My goal is to break down and cry in class.

JULY 1, 3.53PM: PAY-PER-VIEW

Tyson bit off one of Holyfield's ears.

JULY 22, 1.28PM: SPLASH DOWN

3am last night we got picture lock. Picture lock. The film is seventy-nine and a half minutes of picture, plus one minute and eighteen seconds of titles, plus three to four minutes of credits.

We've arrived.

JULY 30, 2.48PM: COMPLETION FUNDS

Tomorrow Randy Simon, David Godbout, Peter Broderick and Stuart Cornfeld will be sent copies. This is a crucial weekend: we are hoping to get the $40,000 we need to finish the film.

SEPTEMBER 7, 11.01PM: THE TIGHTROPE

Up all night. Nervous. Lots of shit going down. IFC's Next Wave and Peter Broderick have bitten. After looking at 165 no-budgets, they want π to be their first movie – they will provide finishing funds, act as producer's rep, and shepherd the film to release. They are incredibly enthusiastic.

Balancing what they want with what David Godbout wants is a fucking serious handful. Kept me up all night. Twisting and turning. Fucking insane.

When we got David and Randy to invest we had to cede certain controls in deal-making. The executive producers wanted to protect their money. So for the thirty Gs they put in they got some serious power. It sucks, but that's how the man with the pocket book functions.

IFC wants to be the new pimp. They want all the controls. They want to be the Big Daddy. Problem is, the ol' Big Daddy wants his balls licked.

SEPTEMBER 17, 2PM: YOUR FEDEX TRACKING NUMBER IS 314159265358

π went out to Sundance on Monday. I remember when I

finished *Supermarket Sweep*, in 1991, I sent it to Sundance but nothing happened. At that time I didn't know much about the festival. It's amazing how important it has become.

IFC is taking its time.

Sunday night, the night before the IFFM, I turned mine and Eric's double date with two Parisienne women into a graffiti tag-up night. The four of us spent the evening tagging up the streets of NYC with beautiful neon orange πs. Guerilla marketing to spark extra early buzz on the film.

Dan Schrecker got married in New Hampshire. I threw the bachelor party, on a mountain in Maine. I had planned to have a helicopter meet us at the top as a surprise for Dan, and it never showed up, so I'm climbing the fucking mountain talking on a cell phone with all the other guys laughing at me. I'll tell you it's no fun trying to direct something when you're not the director.

SEPTEMBER 23, 1.28PM: KILL THE LAWYERS

Next Wave delivered their contract on Wednesday. It made me furious. Not only did they not weaken on any of their terms, but they also tried to grab *more*. Very, very frustrating. We canceled our Friday morning meeting and we wrote a letter which we delivered on Saturday. Now we are waiting for their response again. Damn, they take their time.

SEPTEMBER 29, 12.30AM: PRIORITIES

Very bad news on top of very bad news. Mom has a malignant tumor in her breast. She called me and told me and I don't know what to do. The good news is that it's been caught very early on and the prognosis is very good. I don't think her health is endangered, but I know this is bad for Dad and everyone else involved. It's very strange because only a short time ago, Dad was diagnosed with prostate cancer. His cancer, too, was caught very early on and the diagnosis is now very good. I spent hours of research on the Internet searching for information on different treatments. Now I'm going to do the same thing for Mom.

It sucks because I know how my dad's mind works. He's a martyr and he feels it's OK if he has to struggle, but I know it's much harder for him if Mom is fighting the battle. Luckily, both my parents are warriors. That's the greatest gift I've ever received. They are warriors and when something is in their way they march right through it. Both of them, I know, will be fine. They are both so future-looking.

It sure puts the universe in perspective. Why am I making films? Why am I doing what I'm doing? In the face of mortality I question everything that I do and everything that I am.

I love them both so dearly. I'm trying to be supportive but I'm scared as shit.

DECEMBER 4, 8.35PM: CLIMAX

A lot has happened since I last wrote two months ago. First, my parents are well on the road to recovery. The other big news came last Monday night at 8pm. We got into Sundance Dramatic Competition. It was an amazing moment. Shock, tears – the whole thang:

On Sunday I had decided to go to my parents' to deal with the pressure. I knew people were gonna start to find out that week, so I decided to hide out.

On Monday I got a call from my friend Whitney at Sundance telling me I should wait by the phone. My heart starts ticking. At this point I know we got something and I'm praying for competition. The day is spent on the phone with our lawyer who is dealing with the Next Wave contract. He tells me one of his clients had heard. Heart pounding – I haven't heard.

At 8pm I'm nearly dying, it's 5pm in LA and I figure

they call all competition people Monday and everyone else on Tuesday. I decide to call Whitney. Her machine. I say that I'm dying here and I want to know what is up. I hang up, and the phone rings.

It's someone named Eric from Sundance. He tells me I have to fax over some info. I'm like, 'Yeah, what for?' He's like, 'You haven't heard?'

'Heard what?' I ask.

'Oh, you're my first first!' he replies. And then he tells me.

At first, I think he's my prankster friend Doug Ellin pulling my leg. I asked him to prove it and tell me Whitney's last name. He says that he's in Park City, and not Santa Monica, and doesn't know Whitney, but then he proceeds to give me my fax number and I start flipping out.

Trevor Groth calls five minutes later and makes it official. The first person I call is Eric. He starts screaming into his phone, 'Competition?!' He can't believe it. I call Sean – he just says, 'No fucking way,' three times in a monotone voice and then starts laughing. I hang up on him still laughing.

My parents. Where are my parents? They went on a Shiva call. I decide to call the mourner's house. I call 411 and get the number. I call. The mourner answers. I calmly and respectfully ask them for my mom. My mom comes to the phone:

'Darren? Is everything alright?' she asks.

'Come home.' I'm blunt.

'What's the matter?' She's concerned.

'Just come home now!' I try to stay calm. I can't tell them over the phone, in the mourner's house. It's disrespectful.

'OK.'

I pace, waiting for them to show up. Chills, tears. I hear the car pull up. Rush to the door and greet them.

'What happened to the car?' My dad is sure I wrecked it, that's why I called.

My reply: 'Sundance . . . Competition.'

My parents – who had no idea what either of those words meant six months ago – are ecstatic and screaming. My dad starts pulling out his hair. No one can believe it.

I grab a cab into the city. Whoever can make it rushes to a vodka bar and we have a ridiculous time. Vogel and his wife Jordy, Oren and his wife, Fabiana, Jeremy Dawson, Godbout, Rachel, Eric, Sean. It's a massive scene. We call Matty on his cell phone. He's getting on a plane in Colorado. As always, he's the only one to remain cool.

The best part of the night is that every once in awhile everyone starts clapping and applauding. Not for any particular person or for any particular reason. We clapped just for ourselves. We had done it. We had made the film and we were recognized.

By the way: now we need to get the fucking film done. Fast.

DECEMBER 7, 2.39PM: PRINCE VALIUM

Tim Brennan, the negative cutter, is turning into a nightmare. He's held up the film for weeks now. First he is four months late on delivery. It's too late to pull the job from him, so I jump in. I take a train an hour out to his abode in Forest Hills, Queens.

The guy lives in a tiny one-bedroom apartment with his wife and two kids. He is literally cutting the film in his living room. Open boxes of cereal, dirty dishes, boxes upon boxes of old paperbacks and personal files, and then, oh yes, there was my film. He has an air filter on his table and I ask him if it works – he says yes, but that he has to get a new one because he hasn't been able to buy filters for this one for the last five years.

His computer is an antique. My gut response was to flip out and kill this man. But, we must work with him, so I calmed down and focused on getting the job done.

The last three days I've gone out there and stood over his shoulder. We found a splicer in the city and I hired an assistant, Vicki, who starts today. A nightmare, but I think it will be done by Monday the 8th, giving Cineric two weeks to do the blow-up

I haven't slept for the past week. For the first time I question if we'll get a print in time for Sundance. It would be just a little bit humiliating to be the first film that got into Sundance that didn't show up. Thoughts like these keep me awake at night.

Next Wave deal is still dragging. Eric gave them an ultimatum. Tonight either they're in or not.

Last night, we did our first press. Mom threw a party for the $100 investors, and CBS News and the *Daily News* came. It was silly being photographed and videoed, but I did what was necessary and it was a good warm-up. I ain't no Beastie Boy.

DECEMBER 19, 12.20PM: THERE'S NO BUSINESS LIKE SHOW BUSINESS

We walked away from Next Wave. Very hard thing to do, and honestly I am very nervous. I don't know if we can handle Sundance as well without them. The deal finally came down to Music Rights. They wanted the world cleared, but we couldn't afford more than festival rights. We argued that we should not fuck with the film creatively until we have a distributor. They disagreed. Time will tell who's right.

Getting the negative away from Tim Brennan was a scary ordeal. Four months late and covered in dirt, we get the negative and hopefully there aren't many – any – mistakes. So far, the few tests I've seen seem to be alright. If there are any mistakes we won't be able to complete the film in time.

Sundance looms in front of us and we are very excited. Eric is a bit sick, but we are all really driven and pumped. We hired Clein+White to do our publicity and they seem like pros. We will choose a lawyer tomorrow or the next day.

I went to LA last weekend for Randy Simon's π party. It was filled with Hollywood girls and cheesy guys – mostly strangers. A few friends:

I hung with Trevor Groth and Whitney Cook from Sundance. Elizabeth Morse was there, too. I met her and her twin the first night I got to Sundance two years earlier. The next day Eric and I were on the ski slopes snowboarding with two twin blondes. We kept looking at each other wondering if we were hallucinating. The Morse twins have become supportive friends.

My two directing pals Mark Waters and Scott Silver were also there. We have built a great collaboration and support structure between us that's been around since we were buddies in film school in 1993. Mark went on to direct *The House of Yes* and Scott did *johns*.

Randy has a nice house and lots of friends with sports cars and 4 x 4s that stretch for miles and miles down the street.

The best part of LA was dinner with my buddy from high school, Robert, and his pop Richard Cohen. We went to Nobu's LA restaurant and I had one of the great meals of my life. Miso paste on a plate with unagi sauce decoration with a daichu radish in the center, topped with a duck liver, hijiki seaweed and gold flake. Amazing dish after dish after dish.

Agents and lawyers have found my phone number. Lots of pre-Sundance stuff to do. Randy is making cocktail napkins with the π symbol and a huge banner. We will π Park City.

Working hard on the sub-script with Lucas. The new title is 'Proteus'. It's coming to life.

DECEMBER 28, 1997, 1.28AM: RESURRECTION: BIG METAL CANS OF FILM

Friday I watched the video transfer of the first 35mm blow-up slop print. Amazingly, it was all in sync with the sound from a D2 transfer from the Avid.

What this all means is that Tim Brennan's work was ultimately right on, and the film can now be completed without many more hang-ups. Who would have thought it would all work out? Amazing. Prince Valium came through in the end.

Now all that needs to be done is finish the opticals, titles and credits; music; and the mix. The mix starts on Monday and we will be done on January 5, 1998. Meaning: the first composite print will be on January 9, 1998 and the final second print will be on the 12th or 13th. We will fly both prints to Sundance for safety, and screen the second one.

It's gonna be close.

JANUARY 1, 1998, 11.46PM: 3, 2, 1 . . .

Spent New Year's Eve at a party overlooking Times Square. At first it was a real drag, but then it became more interesting as the night rolled on. The party overlooked the 500,000 people waiting for the ball to drop in the freezing cold.

The mix has been interesting. Watching Dominick, our mixer, work is impressive. He is a true artist. His tongue hangs out of the side of his mouth like Michael Jordan flying to the basket; he really works hard with extreme focus.

JANUARY 14, 1998, 11.55PM: RETURN WITH THE ELIXIR

'Pain is temporary, film eternal.' – Anonymous.

Technicolor wasn't giving us the quality we needed. They were undoing all the benefits reversal gave us. The

black and white was muddy. So we changed labs
yesterday. Last night was sleepless.

But have no fear, today's print is gorgeous. The new lab
gave us contrast. They gave us black. They gave us white.
Happily, they didn't give us gray.

So with the print still wet, we will head to Park City
early tomorrow morning. The Sundance Film Festival.
Somehow, it's all come together and we're all very
excited.

Two years of work and five years of preparation have
ended in five reels of 35mm film. The endless dedication
of thirty-odd film-makers and hundreds of supporters has
led to a pile of celluloid running a few seconds over eighty
minutes.

I hope it makes some sense. I hope audiences will dig it.
At this point: I really have no idea what to expect.

Most importantly: both my parents have finished their
treatments. Health at last. They have both beaten the
cancer beast and are fine.

I set my alarm for 6am and try to sleep. Yeah, right . . .

POST SCRIPT

EDITOR'S NOTE:

π had its world première at the Eccles Theater in Park
City, Utah, on January 18, 1998. The Sundance audience
welcomed it with a standing ovation. Two days later
Variety's front page read 'π = $1,000,000.' The film was
bought by Artisan Entertainment for worldwide
distribution. At the awards ceremony, Darren Aronofsky
was presented with the prize for Best Director.

Taking question at Sundance. Eric Watson (left)
and Darren (right).

After the Eccles screening at Sundance. Sonia and Sean.

π

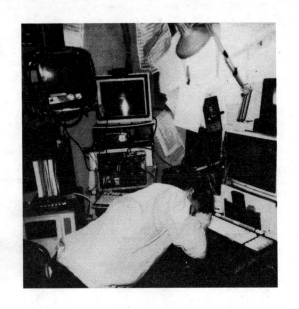

FROM WHITE CRASH CUT TO:

EXTREME CLOSE-UP *of Maximilian Cohen's eyes popping open.*

INT. MAX'S APARTMENT, CHINATOWN FLAT, NEW YORK CITY – NIGHT

Max jolts his head from his desk and tries to orient himself in the darkness. He has intelligent eyes set in an exhausted, good-looking face.

Then, he notices the blood dripping from his nose. Max wipes it.

Max's voice-over begins:

> **MAX**
> (*voice-over*)
> 9.13. Personal note: When I was a little kid my mother told me not to stare into the sun. So once, when I was six, I did.

CUT TO:

INT. BATHROOM – DAWN

A pull-string light flips on. Max examines his bloody nose in the mirror.

> **MAX**
> (*voice-over*)
> The doctors didn't know if my eyes would ever heal. I was terrified. Alone in that darkness. Slowly daylight crept in through the bandages and I could see.

65

Max drinks from the sink and splashes a generous amount of water on to his head and face, cleaning his nose.

He wipes his nose and examines the last remnants of blood on his fingertip. Then, he dips his finger under the tap.

> But something else had changed inside me. That day I had my first headache.

TIGHT SHOT *on Max's hand as three unmarked, circular pills hit his palm. Then, he slams the pills into the back of his mouth. Max replaces the cap on a plastic bottle of unmarked prescription drugs.*

CUT TO:

INT. MAX'S APARTMENT, MAIN ROOM – DAY

Max's room is constantly dark because the windows are blacked out. He flips on his desk lamp.

A tiny ant crawls across his desk. He looks at it for a moment before getting angry and squashing it.

Sitting on the desk are three computer monitors, which Max flips on.

Then, he pops on more lights and more switches. We pull back, revealing that Max's apartment looks more like the inside of a computer than a human's home.

The room is knee-high in computer parts of all shapes and sizes. The walls are covered by circuit boards. Cables hang from the ceiling like vines in a Brazilian rain forest. They all seem to be wired together to form a monstrous homemade computer.

This is Euclid, Max's creation. The computer is alive with sounds and lights.

Max works on Euclid with his solder and drill. He cares for the machine as if it were his dream car.

> **MAX**
> (*voice-over*)
> Heat's been getting to Euclid. Feel it most in the afternoon when I run the set. Have to keep the fans on all night from now on. Otherwise, everything is running top notch. The stack of 286s is now faster than Columbia's computer science department. I spent a couple hundred dollars. Columbia's cost? Half a million?
> (*small snicker*)
> Ha . . .

Max checks the peep-hole on his front door. No one is there. He unbolts the five locks and slides into the hall.

CUT TO:

INT. APARTMENT HALLWAY – DAY

As he secures his apartment, a young girl named Jenna runs up to him. Her mom looks apologetic down the hall.

Jenna's eyes light up and she pulls out her Fisher Price calculator.

> JENNA
> Max, Max! Can we do one?

> MOM
> *(off-screen, over and over again)*
> Jenna! Jenna!

> MAX
> Oh, no.

> JENNA
> What's three hundred and twenty-two times four hundred and ninety-one.

Jenna types it into her calculator. Max finishes locking his door.

                              MAX
                          (*instantly*)
One hundred fifty-eight thousand, a hundred two.
Right?

                             JENNA
                        (*eyes light up*)
Right.

Max heads down the staircase.

                              MOM
Jenna . . .

Jenna screams after him.

                             JENNA
OK, seventy-three divided by twenty-two.

                              MAX
                        (*instantly again*)
Three point three one eight one eight one eight . . .

CUT TO:

EXT. CHINATOWN – DAY

*Max watches people bustle through the busy intersections of
Chinatown. The streets are clogged with people.*

                              MAX
                         (*voice-over*)
12.45. Restate my assumptions. One: Mathematics is
the language of nature. Two: Everything around us
can be represented and understood through numbers.
Three: If you graph the numbers of any system,
patterns emerge.

CUT TO:

EXT. ELECTRONIC MEGA DUMP – DAY

Max scavenges electronic parts as he carefully navigates an endless dump for old and rotting computers.

He unscrews a random IBM board from a keyboard and slides it into his pocket.

    CUT TO:

EXT. PLAYGROUND – DAY

MOVE IN *on Max looking up at something as he reclines on a public bench.*

> **MAX**
> (*voice-over*)
> Therefore: There are patterns everywhere in nature. Evidence: The cycling of disease epidemics. The wax and wane of caribou populations. Sunspot cycles. The rise and fall of the Nile.

MOVE IN *on a tree branch – shaking gently in the wind.*

    SLOW DISSOLVE TO:

EXTREME CLOSE-UP *of stock ticker –*

Bright stock quotes drift across the screen.

> So what about the stock market? A universe of numbers that represents the global economy. Millions of human hands at work . . . billions of minds . . . a vast network screaming with life. An organism. A natural organism.

    CUT OUT TO:

INT. MAX'S APARTMENT – DAY

Max watches the right edge of the screen where the numbers appear. He wants to see what's before that edge . . .

MAX
(*voice-over*)

My hypothesis: Within the stock market, there is a
pattern as well. Right in front of me, hiding behind
the numbers. Always has been. 12.50: Press return.

Max slaps the return button on his computer.

The phone starts ringing. Max eyes it suspiciously.

*Just then, Euclid starts printing results on an old dot matrix
printer.*

Max suspiciously answers the phone.

Hello?

WOMAN'S VOICE
(*on phone*)

Maximilian Cohen, please.

MAX

Yeah?

WOMAN'S VOICE
(*on phone*)

Hi, it's Marcy Dawson. You might remember me,
I'm a partner with the predictive strategy firm Lancet-
Percy.

MAX

I told you already . . .

The printer finishes printing.

MARCY DAWSON
(*on phone*)

I'm sorry I haven't kept in touch but I was hoping that
we could have lunch tomorrow, say one o'clock?

*But before Marcy finishes, Max hangs up. He rips off the
print-out and heads to the front door.*

He checks the peep-hole. His landlady, Mrs Ovadia, is sweeping the hallway stairs humming a turn of the century (the last one, not this one) tune.

Max waits a moment. He tousles his hair. Then, he checks again. She's gone. He opens his locks and releases several bolts.

CUT TO:

INT. MAX'S BUILDING, HALLWAY – DAY

Max locks his front door. Meanwhile, his next-door neighbor, Devi Minstry, a sexy young Indian woman, is just getting home. Max looks away and tries to get his door locked.

She's weighed down by a bunch of bags filled with food.

DEVI

Max, good!

MAX

Hi, Devi.

DEVI

I grabbed you some samosas.

MAX

Great.

Devi heads over to Max with her bags of food. She looks up at Max.

DEVI

Your hair.

Devi hands the bags to Max. Then, she goes to pat down his hair. Max retreats.

MAX

What are you doing?

                              DEVI
          Your hair, you can't go out like that.

                              MAX
          It's fine.

                              DEVI
          Don't worry.

                              MAX
          It's fine.

Devi pats down his hair. Max is humiliated.

                              DEVI
          You need a mom.

Max hands back the bags and heads quickly for the stairs.

                              MAX
          I have to go.

                              DEVI
          Max, wait! Your samosas!

An embarrassed Max takes the bag.

                              MAX
          Thanks.

          CUT TO:

INT. COFFEE SHOP – DAY

*At the counter, Max stirs cream into his coffee. Then, he takes
three pills from the plastic bottle and drops them in his coffee.*

*Max flips past a full-page ad in the paper that reads:
'LANCET-PERCY 86% ACCURACY (ONLY GOD IS
PERFECT).' Max flips the page before he or we can absorb it.*

He compares stock quotes in the Wall Street Journal *against
his print-out.*

                              73

MAX
(*voice-over*)
16.23. Results: Euclid predicts NTC will break a
hundred tomorrow . . . good bet. Other interesting
anomalies. Euclid predicts PRONET settling at sixty-
five and a quarter, a career high.

*Max marks up the paper with lines and diagrams as he
ponders his hits and misses.*

*Then, a puff of cigarette smoke drifts by and succeeds in
bothering Max. He fans it away, when –*

VOICE FROM OFF-SCREEN
Am I bothering you?

Max shrugs and looks over.

*The Voice belongs to Lenny Meyer – a bearded man in his late
twenties sucking on a cigarette.*

*On closer inspection, something is off. It seems that Lenny is an
Orthodox Jew. His yarmulke sticks out slightly from his wide-
brimmed hat and the fringes from his tsi-tsis hang out from the
bottom of his untucked shirt.*

LENNY MEYER
I'm sorry, I'll put it out.
(*which he does*)
The name's Lenny Meyer.

Lenny sticks out his hand. Max responds with a small nod.

And you are?

MAX
Max.

LENNY MEYER
Max?

MAX

Max Cohen.

LENNY MEYER

Cohen!?

(judging)

Jewish?

Max shrugs and turns back to his work.

It's OK.

(joking)

I'm a Jew, too.

(serious)

Do you practice?

MAX

No, I'm not interested in religion.

LENNY MEYER

Have you ever heard of Kabbalah?

                              MAX
No.

                         LENNY MEYER
Jewish mysticism.

                              MAX
Look, I'm kinda busy right here.

                         LENNY MEYER
I understand . . . it's just that right now is a very
exciting moment in our history. Right now is a critical
moment in time.

                              MAX
                           (*sarcastic*)
Really?

                         LENNY MEYER
Yeah, it's very exciting. Have you ever put on tefillin?

*Max has no idea what Lenny's talking about. Lenny pulls a
leather box with black leather straps from his pocket.*

You know tefillin. Yeah, I know it looks strange. It's
an amazing tradition. It has a tremendous amount of
power. It's a mitzvah for all Jewish men to do.
Mitzvahs, good deeds.

*And then, Max notices that his thumb is twitching. He grabs it
self-consciously.*

They purify us and bring us closer to God. You want
to try it?

TIGHT SHOT *on Max's hand as three unmarked, circular pills
hit his palm. Then, he slams the pills into the back of his
mouth. Max replaces the cap on a plastic bottle of unmarked
prescription drugs.*

                         MAX
Shit . . .

                    LENNY MEYER
You all right? You all right, Max?

CUT TO:

INT. MAX'S BATHROOM – NIGHT

Max splashes water on his face.

He pulls a metal vaccination gun out of the medicine cabinet. Then, he loads it with a small bottle of medicine. He rolls up his sleeve, dabs alcohol on his arm, and fires the gun into his arm.

                         MAX
                      (*voice-over*)
17.55. Personal note: Second attack in under twenty-four hours. Administered eighty milligrams promazine HCl and six milligrams sumatripan orally as well as one milligram dihydroergotamine mesylate by subcutaneous injection.

Max slaps himself in the face a few times.

He watches his thumb twitch. And then, pain shoots through him. He grabs the right side of his head, massages it, and pushes it in with his fingers.

In the mirror, he examines the right side of his scalp. He sees nothing.

Ahh . . .

Max walks back into the –

MAIN ROOM

– and sits down in a chair. The lamp is blinding so he snaps it off. Only the bathroom light illuminates the room. He takes a few breaths.

Leave me alone.

Max gags and rubs his head.

Then, the pain seems to disappear. Max looks at his hand which was rubbing his head.

Then, he looks at the front door. The door seems to move.

Something begins knocking on Max's door. The knocking gets louder and louder. Then, the locks begin to unlock.

Now, something starts pounding on the door. The door knob quivers. The locks unbolt. The chains are the only things keeping out the intruder. The door shakes and the chains are strained.

Max is paralyzed with terror.

No! No!

And then the door smashes open. Blinding light fills the room and we crash into the –

BLINDING WHITE VOID.

A moment of silence, then we –

CUT TO:

INT. BATHROOM – DAWN

A phone rings incessantly. Max's eyes pop open. He's scrunched up in a corner of the room, squashed beneath the sink.

His nose is bleeding.

Max crawls into the –

MAIN ROOM

– and picks up the phone. He pinches his nose and tilts his head back.

MARCY DAWSON
(*on phone*)
Mr Cohen. Marcy Dawson here again, from Lancet-Percy. I was just looking over my schedule and I realized I'll be in Chinatown tomorrow around three.

Max heads to the –

FRONT DOOR

– and checks the locks. He is barely listening to Marcy.

The locks seem secure.

(*on phone*)
I would love to stop by and see you. I am so anxious to meet you. It will be worth it – for both of us. How's three sound?

MAX
How'd you get my address?

(*on phone*)
Oh, don't worry, I got your address from Columbia.
So three it is. Looking forward to it.

Max tries to stop her but, before he can, Marcy hangs up. A bewildered Max slowly hangs up.

Max checks the peep-hole – all clear.

Then, he opens his –

CLOSET

– which is filled with random computer parts and boxes.

He pulls a thick neuroscience book from a shelf in the back of the closet. He almost knocks over an old dusty brass microscope on the shelf.

Max flips through the book. It contains old plates illustrating the brain. Max examines some of the diagrams.

CUT TO:

EXT. SOL'S HALLWAY – DAY

Max rings the bell on an apartment door.

A few moments pass, and then, Sol Robeson opens the door.

Sol is a wise-looking man in his early seventies. He walks with difficulty, leaning, out of breath, on a wooden cane.

His arms are covered with faded Russian prison tattoos and he speaks with a thick Eastern European accent. He's happy to see Max.

SOL

Max!

Max is happy to see Sol, but he's a bit bashful and intimidated.

CUT TO:

INT. SOL'S STUDY — MOMENTS LATER

Tight on the Japanese game of Go being played. Sol is white and Max is black. Sol's moves are secure and controlled while Max is hesitant.

Sol's study is packed with worn books and soft sunlight. A bowl of goldfish sits prominently next to the Go board.

Dave Brubeck tunes groove out of antique speakers.

> SOL
> Stop thinking, Max, just feel. Use your intuition.
> *(beat)*
> So what did you think of *Hamlet?*

> MAX
> I didn't get to it.

> SOL
> It's been a month.
> *(knowingly)*
> You haven't taken a single break.

> MAX
> I'm so close.

Sol changes the subject. He feeds his goldfish and points to one of them.

> SOL
> Have you met the new fish my niece bought me? I named her Icarus. After you. My renegade pupil. You fly too high you'll get burned.

Max looks up at Sol.

> I look at you, I see myself thirty years ago. My greatest pupil. Published at sixteen, PhD at twenty.

But life isn't just mathematics, Max. I spent forty
years looking for patterns in Pi, I found nothing.

MAX

You found things . . .

SOL

I found things, but not a pattern.

CUT TO:

INT. MOVING TRAIN – DAY

*Max sits in the corner of a rickety New York City subway car.
The train is almost completely deserted.*

*Max looks down at his hand. He opens his palm and reveals a
black Go chip.*

MAX.
(voice-over)

Not a pattern. 11.22. Personal note: Sol died a little
when he stopped research on Pi. It wasn't just the
stroke, he stopped caring. How could he stop when
he was so close to seeing Pi for what it really is?

*Max notices a Skinny Man in a business suit staring at him.
The man catches Max's eye and looks away, but then, he
quickly looks back, making Max turn away.*

Max looks down at his Wall Street Journal *and draws a circle
with its diameter. Then, he writes '$A = \pi r^2$' and '$C = 2\pi r$'.
Next, he writes, '$\pi = 3.14159 \ldots$'*

How could you stop believing that there is a pattern,
an ordered shape behind those numbers when you
were so close? We see the simplicity of the circle. We
see the maddening complexity of the endless string of
numbers. 3.14 off into infinity.

Suddenly, Max hears someone singing. Max looks up. It is the

Skinny Man and he's singing with passion. It's all very strange to Max who nervously looks away.

Max continues with his work.

And then, the singing stops – mid-verse. Max looks up and the man is gone. Vanished. Max looks around – no one in sight.

CUT TO:

INT. APARTMENT STAIRCASE – DAY

Max heads up the stairs to his apartment. Just then, a toy Slinky appears from nowhere marching down the stairs.

Max stops and waits until the Slinky hits his foot. He picks it up and looks at it.

He looks around, wondering what's going on. Then, Jenna leans out over a railing and starts laughing at Max.

CUT TO:

INT. COFFEE SHOP – DAY

Max sits at the counter frantically looking at the Wall Street Journal. *He plops three pills into his coffee.*

He draws circles and other shapes across the page.

Max is interrupted by a puff of smoke. At the same time, someone touches his shoulder and says:

> LENNY MEYER
> Hey! Max! Lenny Meyer.
> (*motioning to the cigarette*)
> Sorry, I'll put it out.
> (*which he does*)
> So, what do you do?

> MAX
> Um, I work with computers . . . math.

LENNY MEYER
Math? What kind of math?

MAX
Number theory. Research mostly.

LENNY MEYER
No way, I work with numbers myself. I mean, not
traditional . . .
> (*points to his yarmulke*)

I work with the Torah.
> (*awed by the coincidence*)

Amazing.

MAX
> (*passing it off as a coincidence*)

Yeah . . .

LENNY MEYER
Yeah. You know Hebrew is all math. It's all numbers.
Did you know that?

MAX
Hm.

*Lenny pulls out a worn, dog-eared Bible from his pocket. There
are paper slips marking what seems like every other page.
When he opens it up, Max sees that the pages are marked up
by highlighter pens, notes and diagrams.*

Lenny points to the text. Extreme close-up of Hebrew letters.

LENNY MEYER
Here, look . . . the ancient Jews used Hebrew as their
numerical system. Each letter is a number.

*Lenny pulls out a pen and grabs Max's Journal. He writes on
it as he talks:*

Like the Hebrew 'A', *Aleph*, is one. 'B', *Bet*, is two.
You understand? But look at this. The numbers are

interrelated, like take the Hebrew word for father, *Ab*. *Aleph*, *Bet*. One and two equals three. All right? Hebrew word for mother, *Ame*. *Aleph*, *Mem*. One and forty equals forty-one. Sum of three and forty-one: forty-four. Now, the Hebrew word for child is *Yellen*. That's ten, thirty, and four . . . forty-four.

The waitress refills Max's coffee.

The Torah is just a long string of numbers. Some say that it's a code sent to us from God.

MAX
(*mildly impressed*)
That's kind of interesting.

LENNY MEYER
(*proud*)
Yeah, that's just kid's stuff. Check this out, OK? The word for the Garden of Eden, *Kadem*. Numerical translation: one forty-four. Now the value of the tree of knowledge . . . in the garden, *Aat Ha Haim*, two thirty-three. One forty-four, two thirty-three. Now you can take those numbers and . . .

MAX
They're Fibonacci numbers.

LENNY MEYER
Huh?

MAX
You know, like, the Fibonacci sequence.

LENNY MEYER
Fibonacci . . . ?

MAX
Fibonacci is an Italian mathematician in the thirteenth century.

86

Lenny lights up a cigarette and takes a drag.

If you divide a hundred and forty-four into two
hundred and thirty-three the result approaches theta.

> ### LENNY MEYER
> Theta?

> ### MAX
> Theta. The Greek symbol for the golden ratio. The
> golden spiral.

Lenny exhales the smoke. Max draws a spiral.

> ### LENNY MEYER
> Wow, I never saw that before. That's the series you
> find in nature. Like the face of a sunflower.

> ### MAX
> Wherever there's spirals.

SLOW MOTION: *Max looks down at his coffee cup. He pours
cream into his coffee. It shoots up and mixes with the black
coffee forming spirals in the mug.*

> ### LENNY MEYER
> You see, there's math everywhere.

Lenny's smoke drifts by Max's eyes.

SLOW MOTION: *Max's POV of smoke spirals spinning in front
of him.*

NORMAL SPEED: *Suddenly, Max stands up and leaves.*

Whoa, hey, Max!

CUT TO:

INT. MAX'S APARTMENT – DAY

*Max draws spirals all over his Wall Street Journal. Then he
takes a thick black marker and draws a giant spiral across the
entire page.*

Max is ecstatic as he pounds code into the computer, takes moments to wake up, drops pills and drinks a ginseng soda.

MAX
(voice-over)

13.26. Restate my assumptions. One: Mathematics is the language of nature. Two: Everything around us can be represented and understood through numbers. Three: If you graph the numbers of any system, patterns emerge. Therefore: There are patterns everywhere in nature.

Max works feverishly: sketching, pounding out code, and downing ginseng soda.

So what about the stock market? A universe of numbers that represents the global economy. Millions of human hands at work . . . billions of minds . . . a vast network screaming with life. An organism. A natural organism. My hypothesis: Within the stock market, there is a pattern. Right in front of me, hiding behind the numbers. Always has been. 10.18: Press return.

Max is about to slap RETURN *but he stops himself – he's nervous.*

Next door, Devi and her boyfriend are making love. He looks at the wall with disdain. Then, he looks back at the screen, shrugs and confidently slaps RETURN *on his keyboard.*

Stock prices float across the screen. Max can't believe his eyes – the quotes are absurd.

Suddenly, a number flashes on to the screen. It blinks on and off a couple of times.

MAX

What the . . .

And then, Euclid crashes. The electricity in Max's room flips off. The numbers on Max's screen fade to black. In darkness:

Shit!

CUT TO:

TIGHT *on a fuse box.*

Max removes a fuse. He replaces it with a penny.

(*voice-over*)
10.28. Results: Bullshit. Euclid predicts AAR at six and a half. AAR hasn't been beneath forty in twenty years. Explanations for anomaly: Human error.

CUT TO:

MAX'S ROOM

Max tries to reboot Euclid, but nothing happens. He tries a second time, he tries repeatedly, but nothing happens.

Max puts on a pair of latex gloves. He dons a surgical mask. He climbs up to a loft above his monitors. A glass case, fed cool air by a vent tube, encases some computer parts. He carefully removes the front glass cover.

When he gets it off he's stunned. Not only have the chips melted down, but a strange gooey, gel-like substance covers the board.

MAX

Shit.

Then, Max spots a single ant crawling over the chips. Max crushes it between his fingers.

Max grabs his face, frustrated.

Suddenly, he angrily throws Euclid's mainframe on to the ground. It lands with a smash!

Then, he jumps on the smashed mainframe. He collapses on to his bed and covers his face. A moment later:

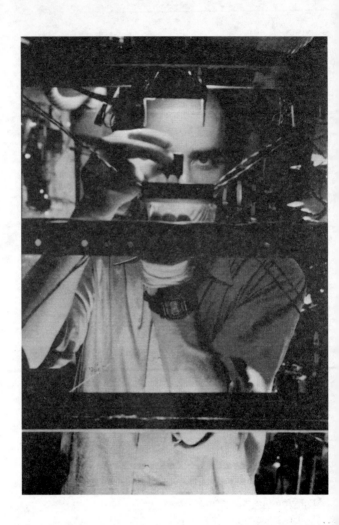

(*voice-over*)
11.11. Results: Failed treatments to date . . .

DISSOLVE TO:

EXT. PLAYGROUND – DAY

TIGHT *on a tree branch shaking manically in the wind.*

Max sits on a park bench watching the branch shake. It terrifies him.

He pulls out the print-out of his picks and examines them.

> MAX
> (*voice-over*)
> . . . Beta-blockers, calcium channel blockers, adrenalin injections, high-dose ibuprofen, steroids, trager metasitics, violent exercise, cafergot suppositories, caffeine, acupuncture, marijuana, percodan, Midrin, Tenormin, Sansert, homeopathics. No results. No results.

He crumples up his picks and tosses them into a public trash can.

CUT TO:

INT. SOL'S STUDY – DAY

Sol and Max play Go. Sol is peaceful while Max is distant.

Max plays a piece absently. Sol counters with a deafening atari. Max whispers:

> MAX
> Euclid crashed. I lost all my data, my hardware.

> SOL
> Your mainframe?

MAX

Burnt . . .

SOL

What happened?

MAX

First I got these crazy picks. Then, it spit out this long
string of numbers. I never saw anything like it and
then it fries. The whole machine just crashed.

SOL

You have a print-out?

MAX

Of what?

SOL

Of the picks, the number?

MAX

I threw it out.

SOL

What was the number it spit out?

MAX

I don't know, just a long string of digits.

SOL

How many?

MAX

I don't know.

SOL
(intense)

What is it, a hundred, a thousand, two hundred and
sixteen!? How many?

MAX

Probably around two hundred.

Why?

                         SOL
                        (beat)
. . . I dealt with some bugs back in my Pi days. I was
wondering if it was similar to one I ran into.

Sol begins to feed his fish. He points to one.

Have you met Archimedes? The one with the black
spot. You see?

Max reluctantly looks down at the fish.

You remember Archimedes of Syracuse? The King
asks Archimedes to determine if a present he's
received is actually solid gold. Unsolved problem at
the time. It tortures the great Greek mathematician
for weeks. Insomnia haunts him and he twists and
turns on his bed for nights on end. Finally, his equally
exhausted wife, she's forced to share a bed with this
genius, convinces him to take a bath, to relax. While
he's entering the tub . . .

Sol places his pinky finger into the fish tank.

. . . Archimedes notices the bathwater rise.
Displacement. A way to determine volume. And thus,
a way to determine density, weight over volume. And,
thus, Archimedes solves the problem. He screams
'Eureka!' and is so overwhelmed he runs dripping
naked through the streets to the King's palace to
report his discovery. Now, what's the moral of the
story?

                        MAX
That a breakthrough will come . . .

Wrong. The point of the story is the wife. You listen to your wife, she will give you perspective. Meaning, you need a break, you have to take a bath, or you will get nowhere. There will be no order, only chaos. Go home, Max, and you take a bath.

CUT TO:

EXT. PUBLIC BENCH – LATER

Max waits for his train on an empty platform.

Just then, he hears a dripping sound. Max looks up and notices something across the tracks on the other platform. He can't quite make it out because his vision is blocked by columns.

He gets up and spots a Young Hasidic Man staring at him.

Blood drips from his hand. Max doesn't know what to make of it.

A train swishes by –

CUT TO:

INT. MOVING TRAIN – LATER

He checks out a few of the other passengers. Then, he notices a Skinny Man reading a newspaper across from him.

The headline reads: 'MARKET TAKES A NOSE-DIVE'. Max jumps up and approaches the man.

MAX
Excuse me, can I take a look at the paper?

Max grabs the paper. He scans the article. Then, he quickly turns to the listings. His finger barrels down a column. It stops at ABR.

(out of breath)
My God. My God. Six and a half.

SKINNY MAN

Hey! Hey, the paper please!

Max hands the paper back and looks at the man for the first time. It is the Skinny Man he saw earlier.

Max gets suspicious and moves into the next car.

At Grand Street:

Max exits. He notices that the Skinny Man gets off – one car down – as well.

He hustles towards the exit. As he's about to turn a corner he looks back. The man seems to be following him.

He dodges around a corner and heads up a staircase.

CUT TO:

EXT. TRAIN STATION – DAY

He seems to have lost him, when he notices a businesswoman with a pretty face heading right towards him. This is Marcy Dawson.

MARCY DAWSON

Mr Cohen! Perfect timing.

Marcy sticks out her hand. Max, not knowing what else to do, shakes it.

I was just waiting for you but I thought you stood me up, so I was going to head home.

MAX

Who are you?

MARCY DAWSON

Oh . . . Marcy Dawson. From Lancet-Percy. We were supposed to meet at three.

> MAX
>
> It's really not a good time . . .

Marcy hasn't let go of Max's hand. She guides him towards a large black stretch limo that's just pulled up.

> MARCY DAWSON
>
> I can't tell you what a pleasure it is to finally meet you. I've studied your papers for years.

Max looks behind him. Coming up the stairs is the Skinny Man.

Max gets nervous.

> MAX
>
> Excuse me but I . . .

> MARCY DAWSON
>
> Listen, why don't we take a spin in the limo?

> MAX
>
> I can't, I'm sorry.

> MARCY DAWSON
>
> Mr Cohen, please . . .

Max attempts to pull away but Marcy is firm on leading him to the car. Meanwhile, the Skinny Man is heading right at them.

Max yanks his arm free and runs away. He whips around a corner.

CUT TO:

INT. BODEGA – DAY

Max barrels into the grocery store and buys a Journal. *He heads to the back of the store and lays the paper across the juice section. Max checks the listing.*

                              MAX

Yes! Yes!

Then, he notices one of the bodega owners staring at him.

    CUT TO:

EXT. PLAYGROUND – LATE AFTERNOON

Max sifts through the trash can where he threw out his picks from yesterday. Frustrated, he dumps the trash on to the sidewalk and starts looking through it.

Mrs Ovadia watches him. Max sees her, and is embarrassed for a moment.

                              MAX

I just . . . threw out something. I didn't realize I needed it.

                          MRS OVADIA

Humph.

                              MAX

Just a print-out. I, uh, lost my data . . .

Max looks back at the trash as Mrs Ovadia runs off. Max kicks the trash can and heads home.

    CUT TO:

EXT. OUTSIDE MAX'S BUILDING – LATE AFTERNOON

Max watches Marcy get out of the limo and call to Mrs Ovadia.

Max backs away and smacks into someone. It's Lenny Meyer – the young Jewish man.

Max jumps back in fear.

LENNY MEYER

Whoa, Wha-Hey! How you doing? Lenny Meyer.

Max tries to pass him quickly.

Where you going?

MAX

Just up there.

LENNY MEYER

You gotta minute? You want to try tefillin?

MAX

No, not right now.

Max turns around and notices Marcy talking to Mrs Ovadia. Mrs Ovadia points up the street towards him.

LENNY MEYER

I gotta car, right over here. It'll take one second, we can cruise over to the shul . . .

MAX

You gotta car?

LENNY MEYER

Yeah, yeah, right over there. See. That's my friend, Ephraim.

We swing around with Max and see a station wagon. Ephraim sits in the passenger seat. He's a big-boned, bearded, Orthodox Jew.

MAX

All right, let's go.

LENNY MEYER

Great . . .

They head for the station wagon.

CUT TO:

INT. BASEMENT, SHUL – NIGHT

The synagogue is a claustrophobic, fluorescent-lit room in general disarray. Two rooms of imitation-wooden pews face a makeshift altar and ark. Young Hasidic men study texts. Some work alone, reading and dovening. Others are in small groups sharing in heated discussions.

Lenny wraps the tefillin around Max's arm. Max just wants to get out of there. Ephraim prays in the background.

> **LENNY MEYER**
> When you told me your name was Max Cohen, I didn't realize you were *the* Max Cohen. Your work's revolutionary, you know that? It's inspired the work that we do.

> **MAX**
> It has?

> **LENNY MEYER**
> Yes, very much. The only difference is, we're not looking at the stock market. Now go ahead, wrap that around your hand. We're searching for a pattern in the Torah.

Lenny finishes wrapping Max's arm. He reaches for another box and strap.

> **MAX**
> What kind of pattern?

> **LENNY MEYER**
> We're not sure. All we know is that it's two hundred and sixteen digits long.

Max, stunned, looks at Lenny.

> All right, stand up.

                         MAX
                      (*coolly*)
          Two hundred and sixteen?

                      LENNY MEYER
          That's right. Stand up, Max. Come on, stand up. It's
          all right. This one just goes on your head.

                         MAX
          Two hundred and sixteen?

*Lenny places the other tefillin over Max's head. Max collects
himself.*

                      LENNY MEYER
          Shhhhhh. Now we're going to say a little prayer
          together, repeat after me. *Shema Yisrael.*

Bewildered, Max does.

     CUT TO:

EXT. SOL'S APARTMENT – DAWN

Max firmly rings Sol's bell.

     CUT TO:

INT. SOL'S KITCHEN – MOMENTS LATER

*Max sits at the kitchen table while Sol heats up a pot of tea.
Max is shaking.*

                         SOL
          Now, what's up, Max?

                         MAX
          What is this two hundred and sixteen number, Sol?

                         SOL
          Excuse me?

MAX

You asked me if I had seen a two hundred and
sixteen-digit number, right?

SOL

Oh, yeah. You mean the bug. I ran into it working on
Pi.

MAX

What do you mean ran into it?

SOL

Max, what is this all about?

MAX

There are these religious Jews I've been talking to . . .

SOL

Religious Jews?

MAX

Yeah, you know, Hasids. The guys with the beards.

SOL

I know what they are.

MAX

I met one in a coffee shop. It turns out the guy is a
number theorist. The Torah is his data set. He tells
me that they're looking for a two hundred and
sixteen-digit number in the Torah.

SOL

Really? What's it mean to them?

MAX

They say they don't know, but that's crazy. I mean,
what are the odds . . .

SOL

Ah, c'mon! It's just a coincidence.

MAX

There's something else, though.

SOL

What?

MAX

You remember those weird stock picks I got?

SOL

Yesterday's stock picks?

MAX

Right. Well, it turns out that they were correct. I hit two picks on the nose. Smack on the nose, Sol.

SOL
(surprised)

Hmmm.

MAX

Something's going on, and it has to do with that number. There's an answer in that number.

SOL

Max, it's a bug.

MAX

No, it's a pattern. A pattern is in that number.

SOL

Come with me.

CUT TO:

INT. SOL'S STUDY – MOMENTS LATER

Sol and Max sit on either side of an empty Go board.

SOL

Listen to me. The Ancient Japanese considered the Go board to be a microcosm of the universe.

Although when it is empty it appears to be simple and ordered, the possibilities of gameplay are endless. They say that no two Go games have ever been alike. Just like snowflakes. So, the Go board actually represents an extremely complex and chaotic universe. That is the truth of our world, Max. It can't be easily summed up with math. There is no simple pattern.

MAX

But, as a Go game progresses, the possibilities become smaller and smaller. The board does take on order. Soon, all moves are predictable.

SOL

So?

MAX

So, maybe, even though we're not sophisticated enough to be aware of it, there is an underlying order . . . a pattern, beneath every Go game. Maybe that pattern is like the pattern in the market, in the Torah. The two sixteen number.

SOL

This is insanity, Max.

MAX

Or maybe it's genius. I have to get that number.

SOL

Hold on, you have to slow down. You're losing it, you have to take a breath. Listen to yourself. You're connecting a computer bug I had, with a computer bug you might have had, and some religious hogwash. If you want to find the number two sixteen in the world you'll be able to pull it out of anywhere. Two hundred and sixteen steps from your street corner to your front door. Two hundred and sixteen seconds you spend riding on the elevator. When your mind becomes obsessed with anything it will filter everything else out and find examples of that thing everywhere. Three hundred and twenty, four hundred and fifty, twenty-two. Whatever! You've chosen two hundred sixteen and you'll find it everywhere in nature. But, Max, as soon as you discard scientific rigor you are no longer a mathematician. You become a numerologist. What you need to do is take a break from your research. You need it. You deserve it. Here's a hundred dollars, I want you to take it. If you won't take it, borrow it. Either way, take a break. Spend it however you like as long as it falls in the category of vacation. Real world stuff, OK. No math.

Max looks at his hands.

Just try it. In a week you'll laugh about this. C'mon, Max. Think about it!

Max gives a half nod.

CUT TO:

EXT. SOL'S APARTMENT – MORNING

Max rushes to the subway when a honking horn stops him. A limo pulls up next to him. Marcy Dawson jumps out of the car.

MARCY DAWSON
Mr Cohen? Mr Cohen? Please stop for a second. Mr Cohen?

Max stops and faces Marcy.

MAX
Damn it already! Stop following me. I'm sick of you following me. I'm not interested in your money. I'm searching for a way to understand our world. I'm

searching for perfection. I don't deal with petty
materialists like you!

I'm sorry. I'm very sorry. I admit I've been a bit too
aggressive. But all I ask is for five minutes of your
time. Here . . .

Marcy hands Max a metal stopwatch.

. . . a stopwatch. Already ticking. Allow me the four
and a half minutes left. Let me tell you what I want.
Let me tell you what I can offer you. Afterwards, if
you don't want to talk to me, then fine, we part as
friends and I promise that you will never see me
again. That's fair, isn't it?

MAX
(*after a moment, he looks at the stopwatch*)
Go.

MARCY DAWSON
Good. It's funny, even though we have different aims
and different goals we're actually incredibly alike. We
both seek the same thing – perfection. I know . . .

clearly we're seeking different types of perfection, but
that is what makes us perfect candidates for a fruitful
partnership. If you let me, I can be your greatest ally.
Take the acacia tree . . . in East Africa. It is the most
prevalent plant in all of Kenya because it has managed
to secure its niche by defeating its major predator, the
giraffe. To accomplish this, the tree has made a
contract with a highly specialized red ant. The tree has
evolved giant spores which act as housing for the ants.
In return for shelter, the ants supply defense. When a
giraffe starts to eat the tree's leaves, the shaking branch
acts like an alarm. The ants charge out and secrete an
acid on to the giraffe's tongue. The giraffe learns its
lesson and never returns. Without each other, the tree
would be picked dry and the ants would have no shade
from the brutal African sun. Both would die. But with
each other, they succeed, they survive, they surpass.
They have different aims, different goals, but they
work together. Max, we would like to establish a
mutually benefiting alliance with you.

MAX
(*handing back the stopwatch*)
I'm not interested.

MARCY DAWSON
Allow me to close.

*The Chauffeur pulls a black suitcase out of the limo and brings
it over.*

As a sign of good faith we wish to offer you this.

MAX
I told you I don't want money.

MARCY DAWSON
The suitcase isn't filled with fifties or gold or
diamonds. Just silicon. A Ming Mecca chip.

                              MAX
                          (*yeah right!*)
            Ming Mecca. They're not declassified.

Max starts to move away.

                         MARCY DAWSON
            You're right. They're not. But Lancet-Percy has
            many friends. Come here, take a look.

*Marcy opens the suitcase. Max starts to look, his eyes go wide
and he reaches to touch it.*

            Can we work together?

*Max eyes the chip. Then, he eyes Marcy suspiciously. Max
smiles:*

                              MAX
                          (*stuttering*)
            What do . . . do . . .

But then, Max notices that his thumb is twitching.

                         MARCY DAWSON
            Beautiful, isn't it? You know how rare . . . Mr Cohen,
            are you OK?

                              MAX
            Yeah, I got to go.

                         MARCY DAWSON
            Mr Cohen. Sir, are you sick?

                              MAX
            Let me think about it . . .

Max trots off.

                         MARCY DAWSON
            What? Mr Cohen!?

CUT TO:

The station is strangely silent. It is also extremely run-down. The tracks are rusted and fucked up. All we hear is the sound of dripping water. The sound is warped and grows and morphs until it's downright scary.

Max sits on a bench sucking down pills. His head begins to hurt. He touches the right side of his scalp and rubs it.

As the blood surges through his head it brings him waves of pain. He gags several times. Then, the pain lets loose and all Max wants to do is die. He smashes the side of his head with his fist.

Across the tracks on the far platform he sees someone.

For a moment Max's pain dissipates. His view is obscured by the columns. Max gets up and sees the Young Hasidic Man – from earlier – staring at him.

The man stares at Max without any emotion. Max notices blood dripping from the man's right hand.

Max looks at the man's face and sees for a split second his own face staring back.

MAX

Hey!

Max charges up a flight of stairs. He crosses a passage over the tracks and flies down the stairs to the other side of the platform.

The man is gone. A pool of blood sits where the man was. Max touches it with his toe. It's sticky. He notices a trail of blood leading off from the pool.

He follows it around a corner where it leads into another corner.

He notices something strange in the shadows. He carefully advances on it. Hiding in the shadows is what looks like a small piece of brain. It seems to be moving slightly.

Max uses a pen in his jacket to touch it carefully.

Suddenly, Max hears a train's honk honk behind him. Max spins around. Nothing is there but silence.

He turns back to the gray matter. He touches it again. Once again, he hears the deafening honk honk. Max spins around but nothing is there.

Frustrated, he pushes his pen deep into the brain – fiber ripping apart.

Suddenly, a train is barreling down on Max. Seconds from impact, Max screams!!!

DISSOLVE TO:

BLINDING WHITE VOID –

We hear two deep, long, sleep-filled breaths and then we –

CUT TO:

INT. SUBWAY TRAIN – DAY

Max's eyes pop open. A Transit Cop is sticking him with a night stick.

> **TRANSIT COP**
> Up, buddy. Coney Island, last stop.

Max sits up. His nose is bleeding. The Transit Cop hands him a tissue.

> Here, for your nose.

Max wipes his nose and looks around nervously.

He sees the rides of Coney Island in the distance.

> CUT TO:

EXT. CONEY ISLAND BEACH – DAY

Max sits on a boulder on a Coney Island jetty. He watches the sea.

Then, Max sees an old man dressed like King Neptune scanning the shore with a rusty metal detector. The old man picks up something. He admires it for a moment before gently setting it back on the ground. Then, Neptune continues his search.

Max wanders over to the place where the old man examined the object. It is a nautilus shell. Max picks it up and looks at it. He sees its natural spiral shape.

Max takes a breath and stares out to the horizon.

> CUT TO:

INT. MAX'S APARTMENT – DAY

Max examines the smashed Euclid mainframe. He uncovers some of the strange filo-like substance. He carefully touches it. Then, he grabs a small pinch of it.

He examines it near a light bulb. He can't guess what it is. He sniffs it. He carefully tastes it with the very tip of his tongue. He still doesn't have a clue.

Max opens his closet. He pulls out his dusty, brass microscope. He dusts it off. Next, he pulls out a slide kit.

Max places the instrument on the window sill. He grabs an old glass slide and puts some of the gooey stuff on it. He slides it under the microscope. He looks into the lens, but doesn't see anything.

He gets up quickly and heads for the –

HALLWAY

– where he looks at Devi's door nervously. He smoothes out his hair, gathers his courage and knocks on her door. Through the door he hears:

> DEVI
> *(off-screen)*

Farrouhk?

> MAX

Um, no, it's Max from next door.

Devi opens the door wearing a sexy nightshirt.

> DEVI

Max, is everything all right?

> MAX

Do you have any iodine?

> DEVI
> *(concerned, she reaches for Max's hands)*

Iodine . . . did you cut yourself?

> MAX
> *(pulling his hands away)*

No. I just need it to stain a slide.

                              DEVI
    Ah, science, the pursuit of knowledge. One second.

She heads to her bathroom. Max waits impatiently.

                          (*off-screen*)
    You surprised me, I thought you were Farrouhk.
    Here we are. What are you examining –
                          (*at the door*)
    – a potato!?

She hands Max a bottle of iodine.

                              MAX
    No, just something from my computer.

    CUT TO:

INT. MAX'S ROOM – MOMENTS LATER

*Max uses his pinky to drip a drop of iodine on the slide. Then,
he slips the glass under the turret.*

*Max catches the low-hanging sun in the microscope's mirror
and reflects it through the sample and up the turret into his
eye.*

Max's POV down the turret of some strange substance.

Max pulls out the slide and looks at it.

*Then, an idea comes to him. He takes out his brain book. He
looks through it until he finds a picture of neurons. He
compares the image to the view through the turret. They look
different but there are similarities.*

*He changes the magnification. At a weaker magnification the
mathematician sees that the cells are grouped in spirals.*

*Max is stunned. He grabs the phone and pulls a business card
out of his pocket. He quickly dials a number.*

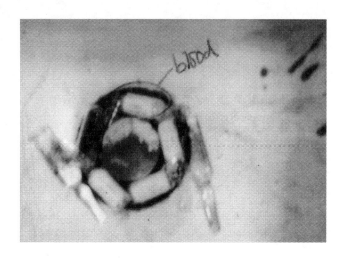

Someone answers with a 'Shalom' on the other end of the line.
Max asks for Lenny Meyer and is put on hold.

> LENNY MEYER
> (*on phone*)
>
> Hello, this is Lenny?

> MAX
>
> Lenny, it's Max Cohen.

> LENNY MEYER
> (*on phone*)
>
> Max! Hey! What are you doing now? Come down,
> we'll hang out.

> MAX
>
> I've was thinking about our conversation the other
> night.

> LENNY MEYER
> (*on phone*)
>
> That's good . . .

MAX

I want to help.

CUT TO:

INT. MAX'S APARTMENT – DAY

Euclid's innards.

Max uses a drill to rip out some old parts. He lays new wire and does some soldering.

He rips down a bunch of old papers and does a general house cleaning.

He also goes to school on the ant population in his apartment. He plants some ant motels and sprays the room with a pest killer.

MAX
(*voice-over*)
4.42. New evidence: Remember Pythagoras. Mathematician, cult leader, Athens, *circa* 500 BCE. Major belief: The universe is made of numbers.

TIGHT *on Max writing 'a:b::b:a+b'.*

Major contribution: The Golden Ratio. Best represented geometrically as the Golden Rectangle. Visually, there exists a graceful equilibrium between the shape's length and width. When it's squared, it leaves a smaller golden rectangle behind with the same unique ratio. The squaring can continue smaller and smaller and smaller. To infinity.

TIGHT *on Max carefully measuring out a golden rectangle.*

A knock at the door draws Max to look through the peep-hole. Devi is outside with a bag of food. Max doesn't answer the door. He just watches her. She knocks again before leaving.

Max returns to his desk.

He draws the rectangle over a copy of Da Vinci's famous drawing of man's anatomy.

The rectangle fits perfectly over Da Vinci's man.

> 11.18. More evidence: Remember Da Vinci. Artist, inventor, sculptor, naturalist, Italy, fifteenth century. Rediscovered the balanced perfection of the Golden Rectangle and penciled it into his masterpieces.

TIGHT *on Max squaring rectangle after rectangle. Then he draws the Golden Spiral through the rectangles.*

> Connecting a curve through the concentric Golden Rectangles, you generate the mythical Golden Spiral.

DISSOLVE FROM DA VINCI TO:

Telescope image of the Milky Way.

Start in tight on the epicenter and pull out to reveal the entire galaxy.

> Pythagoras loved this shape for he found it everywhere in nature. A nautilus shell, ram's horns, whirlpools, tornadoes, our fingerprints, our DNA, and even our Milky Way.

DISSOLVE TO:

EXT. CHINATOWN – DAY

Max wanders through the crowded streets of Chinatown.

> **MAX**
> (*voice-over*)
> 9.22. Personal note: When I was a little kid, my mother told me not to stare into the sun. So once, when I was six, I did. At first, the brightness was overwhelming, but I had seen that before. I kept

looking, forcing myself not to blink. And then the brightness began to dissolve. My pupils shrank to pinholes and everything came into focus. And for a moment, I understood. My new hypothesis: If we're built from spirals, while living in a giant spiral, then everything we put our hands to is infused with the spiral.

DISSOLVE TO:

Montage of mathematical images.

CUT TO:

Pan across new Euclid.

We start on the stock ticker and pull out to reveal a leaner, meaner and more exciting machine.

10.15. Personal note: It's fair to say, I'm stepping out on a limb. But I am on the edge and that's where it happens.

But something is missing. Max holds two wires apart from each other as he contemplates what will connect them.

CUT TO:

EXT. ELECTRONIC MEGA DUMP – DAY

Max wanders helplessly through the dump. There's nothing but junk and more junk.

CUT TO:

EXT. PUBLIC PAY PHONE – DAY

Max eyes Marcy Dawson's business card suspiciously. He dials the number. A Man answers.

MAN'S VOICE
(*on phone*)

Three, eight, two.

MAX

Marcy Dawson.

MAN'S VOICE
(*on phone*)

Who's calling.

MAX

Max Cohen.

MAN'S VOICE
(*on phone*)

Hold on.

*Max is put on hold. He notices a Man in a business suit
watching him. Max turns away.*

MARCY DAWSON
(*on phone*)

Mr Cohen? I'm so happy.

MAX

Look, what do you want for the chip?

MARCY DAWSON
(*on phone*)

You tech guys. I think you know what we want.

MAX

No, I don't.

MARCY DAWSON
(*on phone*)

C'mon, Mr Cohen. We can work together. We can
both profit from this information. We both need each
other to get it, so why not work with us?

I don't know if I'll find anything useful.

We're willing to take the risk.

OK. First, I want you to call off the surveillance.

Done. Anything else?

Yeah, I'm a very private person. Knock on my door and leave the suitcase outside. I don't want to talk to anybody.

How do I know you're home?

I'll knock back.

CUT TO:

INT. COFFEE SHOP – DAY

Max sits at the counter. The Post *headline in front of him reads: 'MARKET DOOMED. PRESIDENT IN PANIC, WORLD LEADERS MET'.*

Max flips to the stock quotes. He can't believe how far things have dovetailed. He shakes his head in disbelief when an envelope appears in front of him. It belongs to Lenny Meyer.

The Torah.

(*orders from waitress*)

Coffee.

                    MAX

What is it?

               LENNY MEYER

In Hebrew characters and numbers.

                    MAX

No, the two hundred and sixteen number.

               LENNY MEYER

I don't know.
               (*beat*)
If you get it, maybe we can figure it out.
               (*changing subject*)
Can you really find it?

                    MAX

If the number's in there I'll find it.

CUT TO:

INT. MAX'S APARTMENT – DUSK

*At his desk he rips open the envelope Lenny Meyer gave him.
He pulls out a black disk and eyes it expectantly.*

Just then, there's a knock on the door. The knock startles him.

A knock again.

*Max looks out the peep-hole and sees nothing. Confused, he
looks down at his thumb. It's not shaking.*

*There's a knock again. Max angrily unlocks the door and
whips it open.*

IN THE HALLWAY –

– is Jenna with her calculator.

Max.

Jenna!?

Can we do one, Max?

Not now, Jenna.

Please, Max.

Max shuts the door.

TIGHT SHOT *of an ant crawling around Max's desk. Max smashes it with a pencil.*

Max paces until there's another knock at the door.

Max peeks through the peep-hole. Two well-dressed large men, Brad and Abe the Babe, wait for the signal. Max knocks and the suits leave.

Then, Max slyly opens up his front door and quickly grabs the black attaché case in front of his door.

Donning a surgical mask and latex gloves, Max opens the case. Sitting in foam is a tiny but beautiful chip. Max studies it with awe.

Max carefully carries the chip over to the new, leaner Euclid. He welds it into Euclid's waiting wires.

Then, Max fires up Euclid. The newly toned machine whirls to life, buzzing like an eager puppy.

MAX

Happy birthday, Euclid.

Then, Max carefully slips the disk into Euclid's drive. Hebrew characters pop on to Euclid's screen. Max pounds in several strings of code lightning fast.

The Hebrew letters suddenly switch to their numerical counterparts. Max toggles between Hebrew and numbers a few times – impressed. He pounds in some code.

Beautiful.

Then, he lifts his hand to slap the return button, but a sudden wave of fear stops him.

(*voice-over*)
18.30. Press RETURN . . .

He gets up and grabs a ginseng soda from the fridge. He takes a sip from the soda and places it on the counter.

Max can hear Devi and Farrouhk starting to make love. Their gentle sounds drift through the wall. Max paces around the room.

(*voice-over*)
18.30. Press RETURN . . .

Max darts over and smacks RETURN. Moments later we see what Max sees:

On the screen is a long string of zeros.

At the bottom of the screen Euclid's cursor blinks, waiting for instructions.

Max smacks RETURN again. He gets the same empty result.

Euclid's cursor blinks, waiting. Max yanks out the disk, crumples it up and throws it behind him.

But then, he notices his thumb twitching. He rubs his scar.

MAX

Ah God . . .

His neighbors' love sounds start to get rough. They're having fun.

Max almost throws up.

CUT TO:

THE BATHROOM –

– where Max dry-heaves in the sink. Then, he forces himself to stand in front of the mirror.

MAX

Help!

He grabs the gun and tries to roll up his sleeve. He can't get it to roll up. Suddenly, he's overwhelmed by pain. He quickly rips his shirt and fires the gun into his arm.

Nothing happens. He checks the barrel – it's empty.

Ohhh . . .

He goes to grab a bottle of medicine but knocks all the bottles into the sink.

He cuts his finger as he grabs one of the broken bottles. He loads the gun and fires the medicine into his arm. A wave of pain and nausea floods in. He grabs another bottle and fires it into his arm. Then, he fires another and another.

Frustrated, he collapses into the mirror.

Stop, please stop.

Slightly sobbing he examines his scalp, pulling his hair apart. He sees something:

So he takes out a pair of scissors and starts removing some hair.

Meanwhile, his neighbors' lovemaking gets more intense. Their screams carry into Max's head.

Max finishes removing a patch of hair from the right side of his

123

head. He has uncovered a light scar on his scalp. He examines it in the mirror.

Then, his neighbors' lovemaking turns outright evil. It sounds like Sodom and Gomorrah next door and Max can barely stand it.

A jolt of pain surges into his head. He grabs his scar as he vomits blood into the sink.

He starts banging his head against the mirror. He bangs his head again and again until the mirror CRACKS!

His neighbors are cumming and their cries of joy are twisted and agonizing.

Fuck You! Fuck You! Fuck You!

The mathematician looks at himself and begins to sob. He reloads the gun and fires it right into the scar on his head, where the pain is coming from.

Max collapses to the ground in complete agony until the bare bulb in the bathroom starts blinking on and off. Suddenly, the pain is gone.

Then, he hears something. It's Euclid, buzzing with life. He gets to his feet and heads into Euclid.

The main monitor is screaming with numbers. The lights in the room flicker on and off like on a disco dance floor. A filo substance billows out of Euclid.

And then, a number pops on to the screen. Max estimates how many digits are on the screen.

It appears to be THE number. Max whacks the PRINT button. Nothing happens. He tries again. Nothing.

So, Max grabs a piece of paper and a pencil. He starts writing down the number. He mumbles each digit as he sees it.

But then, he stops writing. Power surge! He stares at the number. Something clicks in his head. His eyes go wide. He barely musters an –

Oh . . .

We move closer and closer into the number, deeper and deeper into the screen. Until finally a single pixel fills the screen and we're in the –

BLINDING WHITE VOID

– where we hear several deep peaceful breaths.

Then, a fuse blows.

BLACKOUT.

A phone ringing . . . once . . . twice . . . then we hear –

MRS OVADIA
(*off-screen*)
He's alive. His eyes are moving.

DEVI
(off-screen)

Yes hello?

FADE BACK INTO THE MAIN ROOM.

Max's eyes slowly open.

DEVI
(off-screen)

He's busy right now. I'm sorry.

Max is sprawled out in front of Euclid. A large amount of blood, from his nose, is semi-dried out on his chin and chest. Devi hangs up the phone.

Mrs Ovadia and Farrouhk, brandishing a crowbar, stand over him.

MAX

What happened?

DEVI

You were screaming . . .

MRS OVADIA

Who told you you can put extra locks on the door, Mr Cohen?

FARROUHK
(to Mrs Ovadia)

Shhh!

MAX
(suddenly jolting up and remembering)

The number, the number.

Max looks at Euclid. The screen is blank. He looks at the mainframe. It is covered with the filo substance. Then he looks at the piece of paper he wrote the number on. Only a few dozen numbers are on the page. The last number he wrote is barely a scribble.

MRS OVADIA

You're out, you hear me, you're out of here. I've had it with you. Look at all this junk.

Max starts reciting the numbers. Then, he suddenly realizes something. He continues reciting the numbers from memory.

MAX

Four . . . zero . . . seven . . . it's in my head, it's in my head. Somehow I memorized it. I got it up here!

He points to his head.

But what is it?

Mrs Ovadia starts looking at all the junk in the room.

DEVI

Are you OK?

MRS OVADIA

What is this stuff? What does it do?

Max finally realizes that all these strangers are in his womb. He flips.

MAX

Out, out, you have to get out. Get out, get out, it's my room!

FARROUHK
(*to Devi*)

Let's go.

The phone starts ringing, again.

MRS OVADIA

That's it, no way. You're the one out of here, mister.

MAX

Out! Out!

The three neighbors retreat to the front door.

Are you OK?

Out! Get out!

Max slams the door in their faces.

Max rubs his chin and looks around the room. He starts saying the number to himself. He gets more and more excited as he recites each digit.

CUT TO:

INT. COFFEE SHOP – NIGHT

Max stirs cream into his coffee. Then, he pulls out the Journal.

In the clouds of a Lancet-Percy ad – in the Journal *– Max writes down the two hundred and sixteen-digit number. He studies it, examines it, draws on it, tries to figure out what it is.*

Frustrated, Max pops a handful of pills and crumples the paper.

CUT TO:

INT. MAX'S BATHROOM – LATER

Max stares at his bald head in the mirror. All of his hair has been removed. A fleshy scar sits on his scalp above his right ear.

Max ignores the incessantly ringing phone.

Max flips through an old neuroscience book. He examines a few illustrations and finds the part of his brain that's killing him.

MAX
(*voice-over*)
Must be an explanation, must be a reason. Must.

With a thick black marker, he carefully outlines the part of his head that is causing the pain.

INT. MAX'S APARTMENT — LATER

Max sits in his chair staring at the stock market monitor. The phone continues to ring.

Numbers drift by.

A single beam of sunlight leaks through the window and shines on the edge of the screen. Walking along the edge in the sunlight is a tiny ant.

> MAX

Bastard.

Max gets up to squash it. But as he gets closer he suddenly feels mercy. He looks at the ant in awe.

And then, his attention switches to the ticker.

Nineteen and a half. Thirty-nine and a half. Six and three-quarters. Seven and a half. Twelve and a quarter.

Max states the numbers right before they enter on to the screen.

I know these . . . Seven and a quarter. Two and a half . . . oh . . . oh . . .

Max strains to figure out what is going on. Suddenly, he's overwhelmed with fear.

They're going down, down, down. My God. It's gonna crash, it's gonna fucking crash.

CUT TO:

INT. SOL'S APARTMENT — DUSK

Max charges into the room. Sol is looking at his Go board. Sol looks up when Max comes in.

                    SOL
You're early. I was just studying our . . .
                (*noticing Max's head*)
What did you do to yourself?

                    MAX
You lied to me.

                    SOL
I thought you were going to take a break.

                    MAX
You found the two sixteen number in Pi, didn't you?
You saw it.

Sol doesn't respond.

I saw it, Sol. I don't know what happened, but I know
things. The market is going to crash. It's going to
crash. It hasn't yet, but I know it will. I saw it, Sol.
What is it, Sol? What's the number?

Sol sighs. He looks down at the board and collects himself.

                    SOL
You have it?

                    MAX
It's in my head!

                    SOL
                (*leveling with Max*)
OK, sit down.

Max does.

I gave up before I pinpointed it. But my guess is that
certain problems cause computers to get stuck in a
particular loop. The loop leads to meltdown, but
right before they crash they . . . they become 'aware'
of their own structure. The computer has a sense of

its own silicon nature and it prints out its
ingredients.

MAX

The computer becomes conscious?

SOL

In some ways . . . I guess . . .

MAX
(*to himself*)
Studying the pattern made Euclid conscious of itself.
Before it died it spit out the number. That
consciousness is the number.

SOL

No, Max, it's only a nasty bug.

MAX

It's more than that.

SOL

No it's not. It's a dead end. There's nothing there.

MAX

It's a door, Sol. A door.

SOL

A door in front of a cliff. You're driving yourself over
the edge. You need to stop.

MAX

Stop? How can I stop? I'm this close.

SOL

The bug doesn't only destroy computers.

MAX

What are you saying?

SOL

Look what it did to your computer. Look what it's doing to you.

Max doesn't respond.

It's killing you. Leave it unknown.

MAX
(*clarity*)
You were afraid of it. That's why you quit.

SOL

Max, I got burnt.

MAX

C'mon, Sol.

SOL

It caused my stroke.

MAX

That's bullshit. It's math, numbers, ideas. Mathematicians are supposed to go out to the edge. You taught me that!

SOL

Max, there's more than math! There's a whole world . . .

MAX

That's where discoveries happen. We have to go out there alone, all alone, no one can accompany us. We have to search the edge. We have to risk it all. But you ran from it. You're a coward.

SOL

Max, it's death!

Max stands up and screams down at Sol.

MAX

You can't tell me what it is. You don't know. You've retreated to your goldfish, to your books, to your Go, but you're not satisfied.

Sol grabs his cane and whacks the Go board.

SOL

Get out! Max, get out!

MAX

I want to understand it. I want to know!

Sol swings his cane as Max heads for the door.

SOL

Out!

CUT TO:

INT. SUBWAY, PORT AUTHORITY – NIGHT

Max paces on a downtown train as it pulls into 42nd Street.

Through the open doors, Max notices a Young Photographer in jeans and a leather photographing him from the uptown platform.

Max is enraged and screams at him. The man ducks behind a column but a few moments later he's back snapping pictures.

MAX

Hey!

The doors start to shut, but Max uses his body to get off the train.

The Photographer sees him coming and flees.

Hey! Stop!

Max follows the man's movement on his platform. When the young lad shoots up the exit stairs, Max does so as well.

Max catches a glimpse of his foe entering the catacombs heading towards Times Square. Max pursues.

Max chases him down a looooong passage.

But, he loses him at an underground five-way fork in the road. One staircase is Uptown and Queens . . . another is Brooklyn . . . one other is unlabeled.

Still enraged, Max marches forward. Just then, he catches a glimpse of the Photographer exiting the station.

SMASH CUT TO:

EXT. TIMES SQUARE – NEON NIGHT

In the heart of New York, Max spins around searching for his foe.

His frustration mounts until out of the corner of his eye he sees a strange reflection. Not knowing what it is of, he turns around to see the source. The reflection is from a giant brilliant stock ticker – fifty yards long and luminous.

Max stares at the quotes. They are hypnotizing and Max is suddenly calm.

Then, Max has a premonition. He turns and spots the Photographer in front of a porn shop on 8th and 42nd.

CUT TO:

EXT. PORN SHOP, 42ND STREET – NIGHT

Max whacks the Photographer against a backlit image of a Hustler Centerfold. The man screams.

MAX
Who are you working for?

PHOTOGRAPHER
Here, here.

The Photographer hands Max his wallet.

> MAX
> I don't want your wallet. Who sent you?

Max grabs the kid's camera.

> Who the hell sent you!?

> PHOTOGRAPHER
> Wha . . . I'm sorry . . .

> MAX
> Who are you?!

> PHOTOGRAPHER
> I'm . . . a . . . student. I've got an assignment for
> class.

*The Photographer pulls out his student ID. Max looks at it.
Then, he rips out the film – exposing it.*

> MAX
> Leave me alone, damn it. Leave me alone.

Max hands the man back his camera and leaves.

CUT TO:

EXT. MAX'S APARTMENT – NIGHT

*Max heads home in a furious state. Suddenly, he sees two of
Marcy's men blocking his path. It's Brad and Jake and they
don't look happy. Max spins around and sees Marcy Dawson
blocking his exit.*

> MAX
> Marcy? What's the matter?

Max retreats.

> MARCY DAWSON
> Let's take a ride, Max.

I can't, I got work . . .

Max looks back at the tough guys who are almost on top of him.

MARCY DAWSON
We had a deal! Now get in the car!

Marcy releases a vicious slap that nearly knocks Max down.
Max whimpers:

MAX
Don't ever hit . . .

He pushes Marcy aside and darts.

EXT. CITY STREETS – NIGHT

Max flees. Jake and Brad charge after him. They're right on
him – he has a meter or so on them. Max screams for help.

He scurries through a construction site and over a footbridge.

Then, he runs into an all-night –

– BODEGA.

The tough guys chase after him and he gets a bit of a lead in
the narrow aisles. He pleads with the owners for help – nothing
doing.

Jake heads him off and uses his body to block the aisle. But
Max grabs a can of beans and slams it down on the tough
guy's nose. The guy goes down and Max shoots out the exit.

CUT TO:

EXT. UNDERNEATH CAR – NIGHT

Max dives under a car and crawls for terror. He sees two sets of
feet run by. Max starts to relax when he notices a pair of heels
on the other side of the car. Marcy bends down and looks at
him.

MARCY DAWSON

Max. Enough is enough . . .

MAX

Leave me alone. I don't know anything.

Max retreats in the opposite direction. Suddenly, Jake and Brad grab him and drag him out.

Hey! Hey! Help me!

They search him, taking his wallet, keys, everything.

Marcy looks at the guys who shake their heads. She walks over to Max and shows him the front page of the Wall Street Journal. *It reads, 'MARKET CRASHING'.*

MARCY DAWSON

Didn't your mother ever tell you not to play with matches? The market is going to crash, Max.

MAX

I didn't do anything. I didn't play the market.

MARCY DAWSON

But we did.

Marcy pulls out a folded, worn piece of paper. She opens it. It's Max's stock pick that he threw out. Part of THE number is on the page.

You have to be careful where you throw out your trash.

MAX

How could you do that?

MARCY DAWSON

You gave us faulty information. You dangled the carrot, the right picks, but then you only gave us part of the code.

MAX

You selfish, irresponsible cretins. How could you be
so stupid!?

*Marcy jabs Max in his stomach. Max falls to the ground. The
tough guys sit on him.*

MARCY DAWSON

C'mon, Max. This isn't a game anymore. We're
playing on a global scale. We used your code. Foolish
. . . I admit. But we can fix things if we make some
careful picks. Give us the rest of the code so we can
set things right.

MAX

C'mon! I know who you are. You're not gonna save
the world.

MARCY DAWSON

Look, Max . . .

*Marcy nods to Jake who pulls out a gun and points it at Max's
head.*

MAX

My God, what are you doing?

MARCY DAWSON

Information is the private language of capital. We
tried to establish a symbiotic relationship but if you
choose to compete and enter our niche we are forced
to comply with the laws of nature.

*Max thinks for a second. Max thinks hard. He realizes he
can't give them the number.*

MAX

You can't kill me!

MARCY DAWSON

C'mon, Max. You don't get it. I don't give a shit

about you. I only care about what's in your fucking head. If you won't help us help yourself then I'll have only one choice. Destroy the competition. I'll take you out of the game. Survival of the fittest, Max. And we've got the fuckin' gun.

Jake cocks the gun. Max starts to cry.

MAX
You bastards! You stupid bastards!

Suddenly, Jake is whacked with a sawn-off baseball bat. He smashes into the sidewalk. It is Lenny Meyer.

Just then, a station wagon screeches up to the curb. Ephraim and a bunch of other burly Jews jump out.

LENNY MEYER
Max!

Max looks at Lenny. Ephraim grabs Max and pulls him towards the station wagon.

C'mon! C'mon! C'mon! . . .

Ephraim helps Max into the back seat of the wagon and climbs in after him.

Lenny Meyer jumps into the passenger seat and the gray-bearded Yisrael slams on the gas pedal.

INT. LENNY MEYER'S CAR, MOVING – NIGHT

Yisrael yanks the steering wheel to the left, the old station wagon skids around a corner.

LENNY MEYER
Stay down!

Ephraim pushes Max's head down. Yisrael takes another corner sharply.

We've been looking for you.

> MAX

What's going on?

> LENNY MEYER

Do you have the number?

> MAX

What is it?

> LENNY MEYER

Do you have the number?

> MAX

Yeah, I have it!

> LENNY MEYER

You have it! Where is it, Max? Where is the number?!
You have it written down?

> MAX

What is it?

*Lenny nods to Ephraim who starts scavenging through Max's
pockets. Max resists. The other guys hold him down.*

What are you doing!? What the hell are you doing!?

> LENNY MEYER

We're not joking around, Max? Where's the number?

> MAX
> (pushes Ephraim away)

It's not on me. It's in my head.

> LENNY MEYER

You memorized it. Did you give it to them?

> MAX

Who?

LENNY MEYER
Who!? Those Wall Street bastards.

MAX
Why do you care?

LENNY MEYER
Just answer me!

MAX
Screw you!

LENNY MEYER
(*in Hebrew*)

Hit him!

Ephraim pounds Max in the ribs hard – really fucking hard.

(*in Hebrew to the driver*)

Stop the car!

MAX
What are you doing? Let me go.

Yisrael screeches the car to a halt. Lenny spins around in his seat and looks Max in the face.

LENNY MEYER
C'mere. You *listen* to me! You're dealing with something really big now, Max. I don't want to hurt you, so answer me. Did you give it to them?

MAX
They've got part of it. Now, get off me!

LENNY MEYER
Damn it! Damn it! They're using it.

MAX
Using what?

Shut up!

                    MAX

Let go!

*Max chews into Ephraim's hand which is pinning him.
Ephraim screams and lets loose a punch to Max's jaw.*

                LENNY MEYER

No, don't!

*But Lenny is late, and Max's world – as well as ours – goes
black.*

   CUT TO:

INT. MAX'S APARTMENT – NIGHT

*Max stares suspiciously at the bathroom. He slowly picks up his
drill. Wielding it like a hammer, he carefully advances into
the –*

BATHROOM

*– where he looks into the sink. He almost vomits when he sees a
piece of human brain sitting above the drain. Ants swarm
across its surface.*

*Max becomes furious. He whacks it with the drill. Blood flies
up into his face. In a wild rage, he smashes it and punches it.*

*Then, he drops the drill and uses his bare hands to shove the
brain down the drain. Screaming like a madman, he jams it
until it is gone.*

   CUT TO:

INT. BASEMENT, SHUL – DAY

A wise-looking, bearded Hasidic man with benevolent, piercing

eyes stands tenderly over Max. He wears traditional black
clothes. Lenny Meyer paces nervously in the background.

As Max comes through, Rav Cohen speaks.

> RAV COHEN

Max, Max. You're all right. I'm Rabbi Cohen. Cohen
like you. I'm sorry for what Lenny did, he's been
reprimanded. It is not our way. Are you OK?

> MAX

Yeah, yeah.

> RAV COHEN

Everything will be fine, Max. You need to give us the
number. Do you have it?

> MAX

What is it?

> LENNY MEYER
> (*charging over*)

I told you we don't know.

> MAX

You wouldn't be so flipped out if you didn't know.
What's happening to me?

> LENNY MEYER

Give us the number!

> MAX

Screw you!

> RAV COHEN

OK, OK! Lenny, easy! Max, I'll tell you what's going
on. Just calm down.
> (*deep breath*)

The Talmud tells us it began two thousand years ago,
when the Romans destroyed the Second Temple.

MAX

MAX

What are you . . .

RAV COHEN

Just, give me a chance. You'll understand everything
if you listen.

Max takes out his pills and starts feeding himself some.

The Romans also murdered all of our priesthood –
the Cohanim – the Cohens, and with their deaths
they destroyed our greatest secret. In the center of the
great Temple was the holy of holies which was the
heart of Jewish life. This was the earthly residence for
our God. The one God. It contained the Ark of the
Tabernacle which stored the original Ten
Commandments that God gave to Moses. Only one
man could enter this space once a year on the holiest
day of the year – Yom Kippur. On the Day of
Atonement all of Israel would descend upon
Jerusalem to witness the High Cohen's trip into the

holy of holies. If the holy man was pure he would re-
emerge a few moments later and Israel was secured a
prosperous year. It meant that we were one year
closer to the Messianic Age. Closer to the return of
the Garden of Eden. But if he was impure he would
die instantly and it meant that we were doomed. The
High Cohen had a single ritual to perform in the holy
of holies. He had to intone a single word.

*Rav Cohen takes a dramatic pause. Max is anxious to hear
the end of the story.*

MAX

So?

RAV COHEN

That word was the true name of God.

MAX

Yeah . . .

RAV COHEN

The true name, which only the Cohanim knew, was
two hundred and sixteen letters long.

A long beat.

MAX
(incredulous)

You're telling me that the number in my head is the
name of God!?

Wondrously, Max rubs the scar on his head.

RAV COHEN
(passion building)

Yes . . . it's the key into the Messianic Age. As the
Romans burnt the Temple, the Talmud says, the
High Cohen walked into the flames. He took his
secret to the top of the burning building. The heavens

145

opened up and took the key from the priest's outstretched hand. We've been searching for the key ever since. And you may have found it. Now let us find out.

MAX

That's what happened. I saw God.

RAV COHEN

No, no, Max. You're not pure. You can't see God unless you're pure.

MAX

It's more than God . . . it's everything. It's math and science and nature . . . the universe. I saw the universe's DNA.

RAV COHEN

You saw nothing. Only a glimpse.

MAX

I saw everything.

RAV COHEN

There's much more. We can unlock the door with the key. It will show God that we are pure again. He will return us to the Garden.

MAX

Garden? You're not pure. How are you pure? I found it. I'm the one who has the number.

RAV COHEN

Who do you think you are? You are a vessel from our God. You are carrying a delivery that was meant for us.

MAX

It was given to me. It's inside of me. It's changing me.

RAV COHEN

It's killing you. Because you are not ready to receive it.

LENNY MEYER

It will kill you!

MAX

And what will it do to you?

LENNY MEYER

We're pure. Give us the number!

MAX

The number is nothing. You know that!

RAV COHEN

We can use it. We can wield it.

MAX

It's just a number. I'm sure you've written down every two hundred sixteen number. You've translated all of them. You've intoned them all. Haven't you? But what's it gotten you? The number is nothing. It's the meaning. It's the syntax. It's what's between the numbers. If you could understand you would. But it's not for you! I've got it. I understand it. I'm going to see it!

(whispers to Rav Cohen)

Rabbi . . . I was chosen.

CUT TO:

EXT. CITY STREETS – DAY

Max races through the streets of New York. He is wide-eyed.

MAX

(voice-over)

17.13. Personal note: Getting faster, something in the

story within the story, if you stare into space like that, you could go blind, because what can the eye see without the brain? Nothing . . . if the brain can't make a picture and image of what it's seeing . . . it sees nothing . . . it must be just beyond the edge of what I can see, because my brain – my brain is too far behind . . . but my eyes can feel it, and I know that when It happens I will be ready to see past this edge . . . because that's why I came here, and I think, I even think that these headaches, with each drop that has fallen on my brain, the drops that hit so goddamn hard, what if, maybe, they may have been, somehow, a distillation of that . . . ability to see. A little further . . . and I will . . . already I am beginning to see . . .

People fly by Max in a spiraling whirlwind.

EXT. SOL'S APARTMENT – NIGHT

A pumped and excited Max paces the hall as he rings the bell.

The door opens. But it isn't Sol. It's a young beautiful woman wearing a simple black dress. Her name is Jenny Robeson and she is Sol's niece.

JENNY ROBESON

Can I help you?

MAX
(*confused*)

Sol?

JENNY ROBESON

Were you a friend?

MAX

What do you mean?

JENNY ROBESON

He had a second stroke.

Where is he?

Jenny's eyes drop.

No.

Max rushes into Sol's study. The room is covered with Sol's Pi research books. It seems Sol had recently come out of retirement. Max looks at a few of Sol's books. Then, he finds a piece of paper with Sol's handwriting on it. On the paper is THE number. Max slides it into his pocket.

Max looks at the Go board. The pieces are arranged in a giant spiral across the board.

DISSOLVE TO:

INT. MAX'S APARTMENT – DAY

Max sits on his bed staring at Sol's handwritten number. Then, he notices that his thumb is twitching. He drops Sol's note.

MAX

Stop it, please!

He dumps the contents of the bottle of pills into his hand.

Max stops as he prepares to shove the pills down his throat. He looks at the pills. Then, he looks at Euclid around him. He throws the pills and the bottle to the floor. They fall to earth in slow motion.

The room rushes in on Max and so does the pain. It throws him to the ground and he bashes his head against the floor.

(courageously)
No. No. I'm ready. I'm ready! Show me!

Max recites THE number and uses it to get to his feet. The pain rips apart his voice.

Max's pain and anger transform into violence. He attacks Euclid furiously. He recites the number with rage in his voice.

THREE, SEVEN, TWO . . .

He smashes the old computer apart. He tosses his step stool through the mainframe.

Then, he goes to the window and tries to rip off the cardboard covering the glass panes. Nothing doing, so he yanks the entire window wide open.

Sunlight floods the room and throws Max into the –

BLINDING WHITE VOID

– where Max looks around starry-eyed. The pain is gone. Everything is new to Max – even his hands. The stress releases from his brow and his shoulders sag.

Max continues to recite the number. His voice becomes tender and peaceful. As he starts to become part of the void, his voice turns into a whisper and his eyes start to close.

Then, he hears Devi.

>   DEVI
>   (*off-screen*)
> Max. No, Max, no. Are you OK!? Oh my God, Max!

Her voice reaches into the void.

> Stay with me, Max! Breathe, Max. Breathe!

Max looks towards her voice.

> Yes, Max. Listen to me . . .

CUT TO:

INT. MAX'S MAIN ROOM – MOMENTS LATER

Devi leans over Max. Max's eyes are open while he continues to recite the number.

>   DEVI
> Breathe, Max! Breathe. Focus.

Max turns away from Devi and we return to the –

BLINDING WHITE VOID

– where Max continues to recite the number.

>   DEVI
>   (*off-screen*)
> No, Max. No. Stay with me, Max. Stay with me.
> Touch me, Max.

CUT TO:

INT. MAX'S MAIN ROOM – MOMENTS LATER

Devi grabs Max's palm. Max's fingers wrap around her hand. We return to –

BLINDING WHITE VOID

– where Max stops reciting the number. He suddenly opens his fear-filled eyes.

>

                              MAX

No!!! Sol. Sol!

Max reaches out into the void.

MATCH CUT TO:

INT. MAX'S MAIN ROOM – MOMENTS LATER

Max grabs Devi and hugs her. He gasps for air as he collapses into her arms sobbing.

                              MAX

Sol! You were right, Sol! He was right.

Max sobs. He holds on to her for dear life.

And then, he realizes that Devi is not in his arms. He is holding on to himself.

Then, Max notices Sol's note on the ground. He looks at THE number. He collects himself and catches his breath.

CUT TO:

INT. MAX'S BATHROOM – DAY

Max looks at Sol's note. He lights a match and burns it.

Next, he prepares something in the sink.

We hear the whine of a motor. Then, it stops. Max looks at himself in the mirror. He smiles. Then he gets solemn.

                              MAX
                           (voice-over)

17.22. Personal note: When I was a little kid, my mother told me not to stare into the sun. So once, when I was six, I did.

He takes a deep breath. Then, we hear the motor again. Max lifts up his arm. He's holding a drill. He places the bit against the math section of his scalp.

He applies pressure and drills into his brain.

Max collapses.

QUICK CUT TO:

EXT. CITY PLAYGROUND – DAY

TIGHT *on a tree branch gently blowing in the wind.*

Max watches it with peaceful, understanding eyes. He wears a hat on his head.

He listens to the wind in the trees.

Just then, Jenna surprises him with her Fisher Price calculator on hand.

JENNA

Max, Max! Look!

Jenna hands Max a leaf.

Pretty, huh? Can we do one Max, can we?

Max shrugs, not able to say no.

How about two hundred and fifty-five times a hundred and eighty-three.

Jenna types in the number.

Max is about to say no to Jenna, but then he decides to give it a shot.

Max thinks, he really thinks.

Jenna presses the equals button.

I got it! I got it! What's the answer?

But Max doesn't have an answer. For a moment he smiles.

MAX

I dont know. I really don't know. What is it Jenna?

JENNA

Forty-six thousand six hundred and sixty-five.

MAX

Oh.

Max stares at the beautiful child.

JENNA

How about two hundred fifty-five times one hundred eighty-three? I got it! What's the answer?

Max looks up at the tree. Its leaves blow gently in the wind. Peacefully, we:

FADE TO BLACK.

CREDITS

Harvest Filmworks
Truth + Soul
Plantain Films

Present

Sean Gullette

In A Film by Darren Aronofsky

π

EXECUTIVE PRODUCER
Randy Simon

CO-EXECUTIVE PRODUCERS
David Godbout
Tyler Brodie
Jonah S. Smith

CO-PRODUCER
Scott Vogel

CASTING BY
Denise Fitzgerald

ORIGINAL SCORE
Clint Mansell

PRODUCTION DESIGN
Matthew Maraffi

EDITED BY
Oren Sarch

DIRECTOR OF PHOTOGRAPHY
Matthew Libatique

MUSIC SUPERVISOR
Sioux Zimmerman

PRODUCED BY
Eric Watson

WRITTEN AND DIRECTED BY
Darren Aronofsky

THE FILM-MAKERS

CAST

MAXIMILIAN COHEN	Sean Gullette
SOL ROBESON	Mark Margolis
LENNY MEYER	Ben Shenkman
MARCY DAWSON	Pamela Hart
RABBI COHEN	Stephen Pearlman
DEVI	Samia Shoaib
FARROUHK	Ajay Naidu
JENNA	Kristyn Mae-Anne Lao
JENNA'S MOM	Espher Lao Nieves
MRS OVADIA	Joanne Gordon
JENNY ROBESON	Lauren Fox
MOUSTACHELESS MAN	Stanley Herman
PHOTOGRAPHER	Clint Mansell
EPHRAIM	Tom Tumminello
KABBALAH SCHOLARS	Henri Falconi
	Isaac Fried
	Ari Handel
	Oren Sarch
	Lloyd Schwartz
	Richard 'Izzi' Lifschutz
	David Strahlberg
BRAD	Peter Cheyenne
JAKE	David Tawil
MAN PRESENTING SUITCASE	J. C. Islander

MAN DELIVERING SUITCASE	Abraham Aronofsky
TRANSIT COP	Ray Seiden
VOICE OF TRANSIT COP	Scott Franklin
SUNGLASS SUIT	Ted Franklin
MAN WITH SANDWICH	Dan Getz
LIMO DRIVER	Chris Johnson
KING NEPTUNE	Sal Monte

Associate Producer	Scott Franklin
Assistant Producer/ Script Supervisor	Katie King
1st Assistant Director	Lora Zuckerman
Sound Design	Brian Emrich
Consulting Producer	Richard Lifschutz
Story by	Darren Aronofsky, Sean Gullette, and Eric Watson
1st Assistant Camera	Chris Bierlein
2nd Assistant Camera	John Ta
Make-up and Original Special Effects by	Ariyela Wald-Cohain
Sound Recordist	Ken Ishii
Gaffer	Sinclair Smith
Best Boy	Jonah Moran
Key Grip	Trevor Houchen
Art Director	Eileen Butler
Property Master and Wardrobe	Eric 'Shorty' Meyerson
Craft Service	Charlotte Aronofsky Jo Gordon
Schmidty	Joseph Smith

Additional Cinematography by	Chris Bierlein
2nd Assistant Director	Henri Falconi
Additional Camera Operator	Nina Davenport
Additional 1st Assistant Camera	Jonathon Beck
Additional Schmidtys	Chase Palmer

	Chris Weck
	John Fitzpatrick
Ant Wrangler	Nico Tavernise
Production Assistants	Holmar Filipsson
	Howard Simon
Stunt Coordinator	Marc Vivian
Steadi-Cam Operator	Paul Burns
Computer Screen Graphics by	Jeremy Dawson with
	Dan Schrecker
Newspaper graphics designed by	Gagan Sarch, Khalsa
	Graphix Studios
Vaccination Gun designed and built by	Sasha Noe
Additional Graphics by	Sean Gullette
Still photography	Sue Johnson
	Erceila Ferron
Snorri Cam designed by	The Snorri Brothers
Post Production Coordinator	Katie King
Additional Editing	Tatjana Kalinin
Assistant Editor	Fabiana Ferreira
Apprentice Editors	Oliver Lief
	Marc Pholem
	Gagan K. Sarch
	Hilary Scratch
	Anoop S. Virdi
	Meena K. Virdi
	Rebecca Webb
Main Title Sequence and End Credit Design	Jeremy Dawson/Sneak Attack
Credit Ant Wranglers	Matt Dawson and Christina
	Hernandez
Legal Services provided by	Daniel B. Getz
Production Angel	Dolly Hall

Production Mensch	Scott Silver
Production Prophet	Mark Waters
Voice-over written by	Darren Aronofsky and Sean Gullette
Medical Advisors	Alissa Rosen
	Alan Lipp, MD
Judaica Advisors	Richard Lifschutz
	Rabbi Alan Zelenetz
Go Advisors	Barbara Calhoun
	Michael Solomon
	Dan Weiner
Microscope Cinematography Advisor	Gerald McCollam
Shofar Performed by	Adam Burstein
Film Lab	Bono Film & Video
35mm Blow-Up and Optical Effects	Cineric, Inc.
Digital Film Recording	Cineric, Inc.
Positive Cutter	Tim Brennan
Assistant Positive Cutters	Vicki Fredricks
	Darren Aronofsky
Re-recording/Sound Mixer	Dominick Tavella
Dolby Sound Consultant	Tony V. Stevens
Additional Sound Mixing & Recording	Mark Enette
Pre-mixing Supervisor	Joe O'Connell
Mixed at	Sound One Corporation
Pre-mixed at	Blast Digital Audio
Edited at	Palestrini Post Production
	Plantain Films
Insurance provided by	Drift Releasing
Bolex supplied by	Nina Davenport
	Chris Bierlein

Thanks:

Roger Arar
Charlotte, Abraham, and Patti Aronofsky
Rachel Bachner
Jeremy Barber
Bonnie Berkowitz and S.U.N.Y Old Westbury
Tanya Blumstein
Mark and Tony at Broadway Stage
Beth & Ed Brunswick
The Brooklyn Go Club
Burton Snowboards
Whitney Cook
Leonardo Da Vinci
Charlie Degelman
Eddie DeHarp
Sandi DuBowski
Keven Duffy
Steve Fierstadt
Beau Flynn
Ed Flynn
Ted and Caren Franklin
Doug Freeman
Michelle Forman
Formula P.R.
Nikos Glimidakis
Mary Glucksman
Jamie Gold
Marc Grant
Holly Greene
Trevor Groth
David and Margaret Gullette
Tom Heitman
Larry, Lucy and Rachael Hendel
Liora Hendel
Caroline Kaplan
Stephanie Lees
David Levine

Rabbi Abraham Levitsky
Simon Lund
William Mardenborough
Karol Martesko
Hallie Ruth McGonigal
Dan Murphy
Peter Broderick, Tara and Mark at Next Wave
Balazs Nyari
No Time
James and Kellie Lumb
Andrew Osborne
Liana Pai
Eric Person
Mark Picayne
Sheila and John Proctor
Susan and Rose Rubin
Todd Roberts
Stuart Rosenberg
Rob Schmidt
Dan Schrecker
Irving Schwartz
Ellen Schrecker and Marvin Gettleman
Jonah & Billee Sharp
Richard, Jill, and Dan Sheinberg
Amy Silver
Kelly Stevens
Bunny Stivers
David Tames
Ira Tannenbaum
Elizabeth Van Dyke
Joe Viola
Ricardo Vinas
Rick and Melissa Watson
Chad Weiner
Jennifer Weiner
Lloyd and Sheery Weiner
Audrey and Jim Western

Lowell Williams
Dan Winters

Jack Gordon
Anselm and Gundula Grum
Andrew and Teddy Hallman
Donald and Brenda Halperin
Uncle Stanley Herman
Gary and Susan Jacobs
Craig Josephberg
Ken and Carol Katz
Heather Keenan
Steve Kilmeade
Stuart and Karen Levine
Debbie Light
Alan S. Lipp, MD
Gail and Kevin Linden
Phil and Bella Linden
Randy, Keri, and Richard Linden
Alan and Lynn Maisel
Florence Modell
Sheldon and Sheila Pas
Jennie Peabody
David and Leslie Plotsker
Isaac M. Plotsker
Richard and Stephanie Puricelli
Barry Rabkin
Mark Rabkin
Rallo Family
Audrey Roberts
Super-T
Steven Tarantino
Jody and Drew Teora
Chris Varvaro
Brendan Wallace
David Weintraub
Jeff Wittenberg
Wordsound Posse
Marvin and Meryl Young
Leonard and Leona Zeplin

Thanks to our corporate supporters:

Airtime Cellular Rentals, Inc.
Broadway Studios
Blast Digital Audio
Bono Film & Video
Citi Cosmetics
Expendables Plus
ITEX
JTL Cinematography
KiKobo
Materials for the Arts
Mendy's Restaurant and Sports Bar
New York City Mayor's Office for Film and TV
Palestrini Post Production
Screen Actors Guild

Original Score written by Clint Mansell
Performed by Clint Mansell
Courtesy of Nothing Records, Inc.
© 1997 Nothing Records, Inc.
Published by BMG Songs, Inc. (ASCAP)

'I Only Have Eyes for you'
Performed by Stanley Herman
Written by Al Dubin & Harry Warren
Published by WB Music Corp. (ASCAP)

'Drippy'
(Banco De Gaia) © 1997 The Ultimate Recording Co. Ltd.
Performed by Banco De Gaia
Courtesy of Mammoth Records/Planet DogRecords/
The Ultimate Co. Ltd.
Written by Toby Marks (ASCAP)
Published by Notting Hill Music/Wanton Music

'P.E.T.R.O.L.'
(Orbital) © 1996 Internal Records
Written & Produced by P&P Hartnoll
Performed by Orbital

164

Appears courtesy of FFRR
by arrangement with
Sony/ATV Tunes LLC(ASCAP)/Sony/
ATV Music Publishing UK Ltd./PolyGram Film
& TV Music

'Kalpol Intro'
(Autechre) © 1993
Performed by Autechre
Written by Robert J. Brown & Sean A. Booth
Courtesy of Wax Trax! Records Inc.
TVT Records and Warp Records Ltd./ EMI
Used by permission of EMI Virgin Music, Inc. (ASCAP)

'Full Moon Generator'
(Electric Skychurch)
Performed by James Lumb
Written & Produced by James Lumb
Courtesy of Electric Skychurch and Lumpy Spacetime
Music (ASCAP)

'A Low Frequency Inversion Field'
Performed by Spacetime Continuum
Written & Produced by Spacetime Continuum
Courtesy of Astralwerks/Caroline Records, Inc./
Space Monkey Music/BMI

'Some of these Days'
Performed by Joanne Ovadia
Written by Shelton Brooks © 1910

'Angel'
Performed by Massive Attack
Written by Del Naja / Marshall / Vowels / Hinds
Published by Songs Of Polygram International, Inc.
(BMI) / BMG Music Publishing Ltd.
(PRS) Admin. by BMG Songs Inc. (ASCAP)
Massive Attack appears courtesy of Circa Records Ltd.

Soundtrack available on Thrive Records

The events and characters depicted in this motion picture
are fictitious. Any similarity to actual persons, living
or dead is purely coincidental.